AT HOME

WITH MAY AND AXEL VERVOORDT

AT HOME

WITH MAY AND AXEL VERVOORDT

Recipes for Every Season

with Michael Gardner,
and Patrick Vermeulen for the recipes

PHOTOGRAPHY

BY JEAN-PIERRE GABRIEL

Flammarion

CONTENTS

PAGES 4–5: Candlelight illuminates a selection of wildflowers on a round table in the cellar, s'Gravenwezel's old kitchen. Warmed by the fire in winter and naturally cool in the summer, we host many lunches and dinners here. FACING PAGE: A selection of pumpkin-based dishes is ready to be served.

Foreword

AXEL VERVOORDT

"IN COOKING, AS IN ALL THE ARTS,
SIMPLICITY IS THE SIGN OF PERFECTION."
Curnonsky

I met my wife May when she was nineteen and I was twenty-two years old. Even at that time in our lives, we both felt that sharing a meal was an important part of life. That's why, in our earliest moments together, we wanted a feast for every meal. From the simplest dinners to the most festive occasions, May has been as creative with recipes as she has with her ability to conjure up an inspiring ambience around the table.

She has a lot of respect for products and she uses natural, authentic ingredients to define her style. Spices are used in a discreet and fitting way, and they often work as much in the service of healthy digestion as they do in pleasing the palate.

When May prepares a table, the result is like a still-life painting. She has a creative eye and takes a lot of inspiration from the intimate settings presented in old paintings. But like some of the precious objects in paintings, we both believe that rather than displaying objects in a showcase, even rare seventeenth-century silver should be used, with care, in an approachable way and shared at the table to create a memorable experience.

Her collection of cookbooks is also a lifelong inspiration. Recipes prompt her to create new dishes that are an interpretation of her personality and a reflection of her taste. When friends arrive unexpectedly, I'm impressed by her magician-like ability to create a fantastic feast, served on a pleasing table, in a minimum amount of time.

Every night, even when it is just the two of us together, she chooses each detail with care. Whether she prepares a table inside or outside, in the kitchen, the library, or on the terrace, and whether we eat with fine silver cutlery or use rustic utensils made of antique wood, her choices are inspired by the season, the climate, and the mood of the occasion.

FACING PAGE: The winter sun sets as we prepare for our family's annual holiday celebration at tables adorned with amaryllis, glowing candles, and polished silver.

Our time together includes sharing many pleasant breakfasts with baskets of fresh fruit and bread served on a *planche* that looks like a work of art. There is also a particular spot in our garden, under the apple tree, where we often eat. She picks flowers and an assortment of leafy greens from the garden to create a colorful salad that she serves in an earthenware bowl. As always, she uses different plates and dishes to reflect the mood of the season and the light of the day.

For a long time, we have loved food that is both delicious and healthy. For me, the accent was usually on the delicious aspects of taste; May focused on the nutritious value. Finding the right balance is a gift we will always share together.

In the search for balance, she developed a personal style and shared her creations with many friends and family; everybody is always welcome. Patrick Vermeulen, our home chef, has helped May develop her style for many guests and occasions in a very creative and professional way.

May believes that food is energy and has the power to make a person feel better, spiritually as well as physically. The best food should not take a lot of time, as long as it is prepared in the right way. Cooking can be a great pleasure, and just as for a potter who sculpts clay, the skill is a craft and the creation is a work of art.

Food—like freshly cut flowers—offers an ephemeral beauty, because it soon disappears. For our family, ephemeral things are just as important as timeless ones as they give quality to life. Through the memories we've shared around the table, May has nourished my life—and the lives of our children, family, and friends—with an important extra dimension for which I thank her immensely.

FACING PAGE: Peeled parsnips in the kitchen of our chalet in Verbier. Parsnip is an often-forgotten vegetable that's ideal for roasting as a side dish. It also makes a perfect soup.

Introduction

MAY VERVOORDT

"PREPARING NATURAL, HEALTHY FOOD PRESENTED
IN HARMONY AT THE TABLE IS MY IDEA OF HOME."

When my youngest son was seven years old, his teacher gave his class the assignment of preparing a presentation about their families. When Dick introduced our family to his classmates, he talked about his father's interest in art and antiques and shared stories about his older brother Boris. I will always remember what he said about me:

"My mother's name is May. She is tall. She has brown hair. And she never takes us to restaurants because she loves to cook."

Whenever I think of this story it always makes me smile. Even though I was slightly embarrassed at the time, I explained to Dick why we didn't go to restaurants as often as he wanted. For nearly all of my life, the truth is as simple as my seven-year-old son's description: I love to cook.

My interest in preparing natural, healthy food, presented harmoniously at the table, captures the essence of my definition of the home. Cooking and entertaining are an expression of love. Having the opportunity to share this expression with family and friends has been one of the great joys of my life.

Ever since I was eleven or twelve years old, my hobby has been collecting cookbooks. Every moment of my free time as a young girl was spent in the kitchen reading recipes and memorizing ingredients. I enjoyed learning how to prepare the dishes that interested me while teaching myself how to uncover the natural essence of flavors. Sharing my early creations with my parents, brothers, and sisters was a source of a great deal of happiness.

Thinking about our family's life now, it is a bit of a surprise that one of the first books I collected that influenced me was an expansive reference book offering tips for

FACING PAGE: The pleasures of the kitchen start in the garden. For me, there is nothing nicer than seeing the various shades of green that nature produces. Here, an assortment of vegetables—including peas, beans, and carrots—demonstrate the gifts of the garden. One of my favorites (top right) is a naturally simple starter of steamed artichokes served with sunflower seeds, pesto, and asparagus, which may be served lukewarm or at room temperature.

entertaining large groups of people. I read the book cover to cover many times. Even though I was still a teenager, I was fascinated by the quantities and measurements of ingredients. The book explained how many glasses of wine could be served from one bottle and how many could be served from twelve. I learned how much rice a chef needed for 25 people as well as for 125 people. I learned how much time it took to prepare a menu of quail for two hundred guests. As I absorbed every detail, the most important lesson I learned was how the essence of each ingredient contributed to the entire experience of an evening spent sharing the company of others and pleasing people in a very personal way.

"COOKING AND ENTERTAINING ARE AN EXPRESSION OF LOVE."

I believe a hostess has a responsibility to treat every guest like a gift. Creating a pleasant ambience and a balanced menu stimulates the senses as well as overall good health. For me, the best evening dinners are those that resonate with vibrant memories and new feelings that linger for many days after the experience.

My philosophy as a hostess starts with the romantic notion of creating an attractive table surrounded by pleasant guests eating healthy food in an inspiring setting while engaging in lively conversation. With all of these elements, the table becomes life's focal point.

One of the turning points in my life happened when I was nineteen years old. My mother died suddenly. The loss of her presence in our lives broke our hearts. As a way to continue her legacy and nurture the longevity of my father and siblings, I wanted to be sure that the family was well taken care of in her absence. I turned to the warmth of the kitchen with the understanding that food nurtures and sustains life. I put my interest for cooking into practice and prepared many meals for the health and healing of the family.

Around this time, my life changed again when I met my husband, Axel. I was a student at art school and, in the free time between my studies, I organized lunch and dinner for my father and siblings, and then I traveled to Antwerp to prepare dinner for Axel. He was hard at work restoring the sixteenth-century buildings of the Vlaeykensgang, the place that would become the early home of our family and art and antiques business.

At the Vlaeykensgang, we worked closely with clients and friends on interesting projects while sharing long lunches and dinners together. These were busy, productive days and we needed creative, healthy food that added value to those special moments while providing nutrients and energy for the next day.

In the beginning, I loved preparing everything myself. Even after a day of work, being in the kitchen allowed me to refresh my mind and body and focus on preparing

FACING PAGE: An excellent starter or first course, a tray of assorted steamed vegetables served with fresh crab is surrounded by Korean pottery and served for lunch in the cellar. Fresh food presented in a simple way represents a pleasant gesture that welcomes guests and makes them feel at home.

robust, nutritious meals in an efficient way. Food brought awareness to our lives by stimulating the senses and nourishing our bodies.

I couldn't have known then that every lunch and dinner—from intimate lunches for six people to Renaissance-inspired parties for one hundred—were the building blocks for many of the recipe creations that I'm thankful to share here for the first time.

"NATURE'S SIMPLICITY IS THE ULTIMATE SOPHISTICATION."

We lived for fourteen years in the center of Antwerp and, as the business grew, our family moved from Antwerp to s'Gravenwezel. We started a long project to restore each room to its pure, natural character and spent every weekend and summer holiday for two years working at the new home. At the end of those workdays, anyone who helped—the gardeners, carpenters, painters, colleagues, family, and friends—gathered together for a late evening meal. I would cut fresh flowers from the garden, prepare a table on the terrace, and serve a mixed green salad with roasted vegetables and twenty-five grilled fish with herbs.

Our life was growing along with our surroundings, so we were grateful for the opportunity to host more events at home. I began spending a lot more time balancing client projects and, occasionally, as a result, I had to make a call to a caterer when time was short. It became clear that I needed to find the right partner to assist in the kitchen to manage the growing number of engagements.

Soon after, I met chef Patrick Vermeulen. We have now known each other for more than a quarter century and have collaborated for over a decade. He has all of the important skills of a successful chef—confidence, inventive creativity, organization, and nerves of steel—and we shared an interest in food with the same creative approach to natural cuisine.

Additionally, a trip I took to the Henri Chenot center in Italy also influenced me. A close family friend encouraged me to spend a week focused on wellness and detoxifying cuisine. At Chenot, I learned a lot about living a life in balance with the power of food. I learned about the use of proper nutrition and intelligent food combinations to aid digestion and promote well-being. Inspired by my experiences there, I started to incorporate more vegetables, grains, and ayurvedic ingredients, such as turmeric, long black pepper, and cinnamon, into my own creations and experimented with Patrick to develop combinations we could share with friends and family.

Together, we've created a collection of recipes based on taste and simplicity. Our menus use fresh, seasonal ingredients cultivated from the garden with a respect for the true essence of flavor as intended by nature.

FACING PAGE: Sharing food with friends is a timeless gift that delights the palate and inspires memories. Flaky pumpkin tarts are ready to be served on an antique glass tazza, a favorite stemmed serving dish. The crusty texture is necessary and a nice accompaniment to the creamy flavor of pumpkin.

For most occasions, we organize menus using the freshest ingredients possible with balanced food combinations. Together they contribute to an experience that is savory, satisfying, and light.

When we create a menu, we think first of the garden and ask ourselves what is in season. Next we consider our guests and the formality of the event to help inform our choices. We also plan ahead in case there may be any allergies or special considerations for the evening.

For example, we avoid serving two different proteins in the same meal, such as an appetizer with meat followed by a fish entrée; this helps promote healthy digestion. We also don't use flour or any dairy products. Simple decisions like saving the water from boiled vegetables for use as a base for a vinaigrette is part of our conscious efforts to maximize resources for useful results. We have eliminated cream sauces as well as pretentious ingredients, so all of the recipes are accessible for both simple and formal occasions. The recipes also use very little sugar, which we often substitute with a natural sweetener like agave syrup.

I prefer to offer a variety of dishes with subtle connections in taste and flavor, so every dish is carefully considered while always offering guests an enjoyable range of choice. The joy of cooking at home is trying to capture every unique moment of the seasonal garden by presenting the ingredients on the plate in a way that is memorable and timeless.

Following dinner, we offer herbal tea and a selection of desserts in another room. Lime-blossom tea or vervain are both favorites. Desserts are offered on a buffet table so guests can feel free to sample without feeling obliged. I find it is important not to stay seated for too long at the table, so that guests feel comfortable and have the chance to interact with others and relax in a different atmosphere.

From the very beginning through to the present, with Patrick's help, we have been able to translate recipes to meet the scale of both personal and professional events. The work of our company from the offices at the Kanaal now takes us to many places around the world, and yet I always want to ensure that a personal touch remains and that every guest we meet feels a close connection to the experience.

In a given year, we may host hundreds of lunches and dinners. We consider ourselves very fortunate to see thousands of old friends and new friends. Whether it is a breakfast for twenty musicians for our music foundation Inspiratum, a Sunday brunch for fifty at Kanaal, or an opening dinner buffet for an art exhibition in Venice for a few hundred artists, friends, and guests, I always focus on the experience of every guest in the same way that I would when preparing a special dinner for four in the dining room.

FACING PAGE: For a dinner hosted in late autumn at home in one of the side buildings, I collected the season's last offerings from the garden and placed single flowers in a long row of vases to show off their natural beauty. Combined with dried leaves from a walk in the park, the colors of nature help define the style of a table, and a celebratory evening held in honor of a close family friend.

"THE EPHEMERAL BEAUTY OF FLOWERS BRINGS THE VITALITY OF NATURE INTO THE ROOM."

I'm a very visual person and I love to work with my hands. This is one of the reasons why I feel a close connection to nature, which is expressed in many aspects when receiving guests. There are many details in addition to the food that make an evening enjoyable. This includes the presentation of flowers, selection of plates, cutlery, and glassware, and the creation of a pleasant atmosphere in any setting.

The beauty of nature is reflected in the impermanence of flowers. A room filled with objects can be a place of wonder; the use of flowers infuses the room with life. The same way I try to incorporate seasonal ingredients in a dish, I rely on the flower garden to bring the vitality of nature into the room. If there are already flowers somewhere in the room, it is not always necessary to add them to the table, but their presence is important to every occasion.

Instead of twelve flowers in a centerpiece, I prefer a collection of small vases filled with single flowers scattered across the table or throughout a room. Flowers make a setting seem more natural and joyful. The flowers don't have to be from a florist. At times, they can be touches of nature that I've gathered myself; leaves in the autumn or stones from a walk in the park. Even in the absence of flowers, lemons or other fruit add a surprising burst of color in a room as they gleam and pick up the light to enhance the ambience.

In selecting the right plates and serving dishes, I'm often drawn to subtle, natural colors and plates without any patterns or motifs, so the natural creativity of the food remains the focus. There are exceptions, of course, and the truth is I am always looking for new dishes. I love hunting for French and Italian ceramics while traveling around Europe. Axel and I are often on the lookout for pottery and have even started making some of our own.

After a trip to Japan, I was inspired by Japanese stoneware and our hosts' way of presenting food so that each plate was closely associated with the size and flavors of the dish. In the course of the same meal, I often change the plates according to the menu so that the colors, flavors, and visuals are interrelated. The tastes work in harmony with the presentation to create an element of surprise.

From those special times I spent reading the first cookbooks I collected as a young woman, and throughout the years, my experiences with food and entertaining have continued to evolve. I'm humbled by the opportunity to offer the images and recipes collected in this book with you. I hope they inspire many memorable moments shared with family and friends in the creation of harmony at home.

FACING PAGE: Alongside images of two summer tables are portraits of Patrick Vermeulen and myself, capturing moments in the creative process in and around the kitchen. I still remember the thrill of first holding a cookbook in my hand as a teenager. Creating this book was just as exciting. In the orangery, bright bouquets of zinnias share a table with baskets of black cherries. Inspired by the colors of the season, a dinner table in the hall is set with hydrangeas.
PAGES 22–23: An assortment of vegetables is the first course for a spring lunch in the blue and white dining room.

SPRING

A season of rebirth, I cherish the early days of spring and the lengthening of the daylight hours. It's an exciting time and a season that helps define the flavors for the entire year. As early as possible when the weather starts to warm, we make the selection of the vegetables and herbs that we'll grow in the garden each year. Spring is an important time to plan, organize, and discover new tastes. I particularly look forward to harvesting the first carrots and green asparagus and tasting a fresh, crisp salad. Known for its naturally detoxifying qualities, nettle soup is a dish I like to serve late in the season. After having winter meals indoors, I love to have the first lunches outside, under the apple tree. This is the time to use bright lunch and dinner plates to add a burst of color to a table and complement the presentation with cheerful flowers, such as daisies and narcissus.

Facing page: The meadow garden bursts with life. It's always a pleasure for me to witness the garden's growth and rediscover its beauty in spring.

Right: A delicious vegetable that promotes healthy digestion: steamed, young fennel served in a wooden bowl.

Pages 26–27: The first spring lunch under our apple tree with herb-roasted fish and vegetables.

Green Apple, Spinach, Mint, and Gingerroot Juice

SERVES 4

PREPARATION TIME 10 MINUTES

- 4 Granny Smith apples, peeled, cored, and diced
- 4 $\frac{1}{2}$ oz. (125 g) fresh spinach, finely chopped
- 1 celery stalk
- 2 tablespoons finely chopped fresh gingerroot
- 1 fresh lemongrass stalk, finely chopped
- 8 flat-leaf parsley sprigs, finely chopped
- 8 fresh mint leaves, finely chopped

Wash, trim, and dry the spinach, parsley, and mint.
Put all the ingredients into a juicer to extract the juices.

Tomato and Carrot Juice

SERVES 4

PREPARATION TIME 10 MINUTES

- 4 large tomatoes, peeled and diced
- 2 carrots, peeled and diced
- 1 celery stalk, diced
- 1 tablespoon chopped fresh gingerroot
- $\frac{1}{2}$ teaspoon fresh turmeric

Put all the ingredients into a juicer to extract the juices.

Carrot, Apple, and Gingerroot juice

SERVES 4

PREPARATION TIME 10 MINUTES

- 1 lb. (500 g) carrots
- 4 apples (e.g., Pink Lady, Jonagold, Reinette/Rennet)
- 1 large celery stalk
- 1 $\frac{1}{2}$ oz. (40 g) fresh gingerroot
- $\frac{1}{3}$ oz. (10 g) fresh turmeric
- 1 untreated lemon or lime

Wash and dry, but do not peel, the carrots, apples, and celery. Cut them into pieces of equal size.
Peel and finely chop the gingerroot and turmeric.
Peel the lemon or lime *à vif* (see Tip).
Put all the ingredients into a juicer to extract the juices.

Tip: To peel a citrus fruit *à vif*, first cut off the two ends as far as the flesh. Then, using a sharp knife and following the curve of the fruit, remove the peel from successive portions until the segments are free of any pith.

PEA PESTO BRUSCHETTA WITH ASPARAGUS TIPS

SERVES 4

PREPARATION TIME 20 MINUTES

- 3 $^1/_2$ oz. (100 g) peas
- 1 tablespoon pine nuts
- 2 garlic cloves, finely chopped
- 8 basil sprigs
- 1 tablespoon grated Parmesan
- Juice and zest of $^1/_2$ lemon
- 8 fresh mint leaves
- Scant $^1/_2$ cup (100 ml) extra virgin olive oil
- Sea salt and freshly ground black pepper
- 12 slices of whole-wheat baguette
- 12 green asparagus tips
- 2 tablespoons sunflower seeds

To make the pea pesto, put the peas, pine nuts, garlic, basil, Parmesan, lemon juice and zest, mint leaves, and $^1/_3$ cup (80 ml) olive oil into a food processor and blend until thick and creamy. Season with salt and pepper.

Drizzle the bread slices with the rest of the olive oil, season with salt and pepper, and broil under the broiler.

Place the asparagus tips into a pan of boiling, salted water and cook for 8 to 10 minutes. Drain the asparagus tips, let cool, and set aside.

In a skillet, dry-fry the sunflower seeds with some salt and pepper.

Spread the toasted bread slices with the pesto.

Decorate each piece of bread with an asparagus tip and a few toasted sunflower seeds.

TOMATO, BUFFALO MOZZARELLA, AND OLIVE MILLE-FEUILLE

SERVES 4

PREPARATION TIME 30 MINUTES

- 1 puff pastry sheet (8 $^3/_4$ oz./245 g)
- $^1/_3$ cup (80 ml) extra virgin olive oil
- 1 large white onion, finely chopped
- 1 garlic clove, finely chopped
- 2 buffalo mozzarella balls (9 oz./250g)
- Sea salt and freshly ground black pepper
- 1 tablespoon chopped fresh oregano
- 2 beefsteak tomatoes
- 1 $^3/_4$ oz. (50 g) pitted black olives, finely chopped

Preheat the oven to 350°F (180°C/gas 4). Cut 8 × 2 $^1/_4$-in. (7-cm) diameter circles from the puff pastry. Place the pastry circles on a baking sheet, prick lightly with a fork, and cook in the oven for 15 minutes.

Heat 2 tablespoons of the olive oil in a skillet and sweat the onion and garlic until the onion is transparent.

Cut each mozzarella ball into 8 thin slices. Sprinkle the mozzarella slices with salt, pepper, and chopped oregano, and drizzle with olive oil.

Peel the tomatoes and cut into each into 4 thick slices.

Remove the pastry circles from the oven and reduce the oven temperature to 325°F (160°C/gas 3).

Top each cooked pastry circle with the onion and garlic mixture, followed by a slice of mozzarella, a slice of tomato and a second slice of mozzarella. Finally, sprinkle with the chopped olives.

Cook in the oven for 8 minutes.

ABOVE, TOP: These mille-feuilles can be served with a zesty tomato sauce and arugula seasoned with olive oil and a drizzle of lemon juice.
ABOVE, BOTTOM: A wooden side entry gate to the garden is slightly open to reveal a view of the spring awakening after a long winter.

PAGES 32 AND 33: The first, young carrots of the season offer a heavenly taste. Whether eaten raw for their crisp flavor, or seasoned with ayurvedic spices, carrots are a timeless treasure.
ABOVE: I have two weaknesses: I always buy baskets and I can't stop collecting wooden spoons. These spoons made of lemon wood are delightful to use for salads and vinaigrettes.

CARROT, GINGERROOT, AND CORIANDER SALAD

SERVES 4

PREPARATION TIME 20 MINUTES

- 1 bunch (about 1 lb. / 500 g) baby carrots, peeled and sliced diagonally
- 1 tablespoon coriander seeds
- $^1/_4$ cup (60 ml) extra virgin olive oil
- 1 large shallot, chopped
- $^3/_4$ in. (2 cm) fresh gingerroot, peeled and sliced thinly
- 1 pinch of cane sugar (or drop of agave syrup)
- 1 bay leaf
- 1 thyme sprig
- 8 fresh sage leaves
- Sea salt and freshly ground black pepper
- Scant 1 cup (200 ml) vegetable stock
- Juice of 1 orange

Crush the coriander seeds using a pestle and mortar and dry-fry them in a skillet. Remove them from the skillet as soon as they begin to release their aromas to prevent further cooking.
Heat a drizzle of olive oil in a pan and sweat the chopped shallot. Add the coriander seeds and gingerroot, then the carrots, sugar, bay leaf, thyme, and sage. Pour in the vegetable stock and simmer gently, uncovered, until the liquid has evaporated.
Season with salt and pepper.
Mix together the orange juice and the remaining olive oil to dress the salad.

GREEN SALAD WITH ASPARAGUS AND ROMANESCO BROCCOLI

SERVES 4

PREPARATION TIME 30 MINUTES

- 20 green asparagus stalks
- 1 small Romanesco broccoli
- $^2/_3$ cup (160 ml) extra virgin olive oil
- 1 garlic clove, finely chopped
- 1 shallot, finely chopped
- 7 oz. (200 g) baby spinach leaves
- 3 $^1/_2$ oz. (100 g) arugula
- 2 sucrines
- 1 $^1/_4$ cups (1 $^3/_4$ oz./50 g) finely chopped fresh flat-leaf parsley
- 1 $^1/_4$ cups (1 $^3/_4$ oz./50 g) finely chopped fresh chervil
- 1 $^1/_4$ cups (1 $^3/_4$ oz./50 g) finely chopped fresh tarragon
- 2 tablespoons lemon juice
- 1 teaspoon wholegrain mustard
- Sea salt and freshly ground black pepper

Peel the lower parts of the asparagus stalks and cook whole in boiling salted water for 6 minutes, until al dente. Refresh under cold water. Remove the flowerets from the Romanesco broccoli and blanch in the same way for 4–5 minutes.
Heat 2 tablespoons of the oil in a frying pan and sweat the garlic and shallot. Wash and spin or pat dry the spinach, arugula, and sucrine leaves and place in a salad bowl with the chopped herbs, asparagus, Romanesco broccoli and the shallot mixture.
To make the dressing, mix together the remaining olive oil, lemon juice, mustard, and salt and pepper. Pour over the salad and toss. Serve immediately.

Tip: If you can find it in season, you can replace the green asparagus with wild asparagus. This has thinner stalks and is actually part of a different botanical family. The cooking method is similar.

SUCRINE, RADICCHIO, AND GREEN ASPARAGUS

SERVES 4

PREPARATION TIME 25 MINUTES

- 4 sucrines
- 1 small radicchio
- 12 green asparagus stalks
- $1/3$ cup (80 ml) extra virgin olive oil
- 1 shallot, finely chopped
- 1 garlic clove, finely chopped
- 1 teaspoon Dijon mustard
- Juice of $1/2$ lemon
- Leaves from 2 tarragon sprigs, chopped
- Sea salt and freshly ground black pepper

Separate, wash, and spin or pat dry the sucrine leaves. Coarsely chop the radicchio.

Peel the asparagus and cook in boiling salted water for about 8 minutes until al dente, then plunge into iced water. Drain.

Put the salad leaves and asparagus in a bowl.

To make the dressing, heat 1 tablespoon of the oil in a skillet and sweat the shallot and garlic.

In a small bowl or jar, mix together the remaining olive oil, mustard, a drizzle of lemon juice, the chopped tarragon, and shallot and garlic. Season with salt and pepper.

Pour the dressing over the salad and toss.

Tip: Plunging vegetables into iced water stops the effect of the heat of the cooking water and preserves the pigments, including chlorophyll.

A spice that we use in many recipes throughout this book is coriander; an important ingredient that comes from the Middle East and Mediterranean. One great advantage of the coriander plant is that you can eat both the leaf and the seeds. Patrick and I always dry the seeds so that they can be used in ground form, similar to pepper, which is a marvelous seasoning to use with fish. The easiest recipe for delicious fish is to combine the ground seeds of coriander with a little bit of olive oil, coat the fish with this mixture, and cook in the oven, sprinkling the dish with a bit of pepper and salt before serving.

HUMMUS, DRIED TOMATO, AND OLIVE BRUSCHETTA

SERVES 4

PREPARATION TIME 15 MINUTES

- $^{1}/_{2}$ cup (120 ml) extra virgin olive oil
- 12 thin slices of multigrain baguette
- Sea salt and freshly ground black pepper
- 4 dried tomatoes
- 8 large olives, chopped
- 1 small garlic clove, finely chopped
- 12 fresh cilantro leaves, chopped
- $^{1}/_{2}$ cup (3 $^{1}/_{2}$ oz./100 g) hummus (see page 122)
- $^{1}/_{4}$ lemon

Heat half the oil in a skillet and fry the bread slices on both sides until golden. Season with salt and pepper. Drain the fried bread on paper towel.
Soak the dried tomatoes in boiling water for 5 minutes. Drain and let cool. Chop the tomatoes and put in a bowl with the chopped olives and garlic. Season with the remaining olive oil and the cilantro. Spread the fried bread slices with the hummus and top with the olive and tomato mixture. Serve immediately, with a little lemon juice squeezed over.

YOGURT AND FRESH HERB SAUCE

SERVES 4

PREPARATION TIME 10 MINUTES

- 3 oz. (85 g) arugula
- 1 oz. (30 g) baby spinach leaves
- 1 oz. (30 g) fresh flat-leaf parsley
- 1 oz. (30 g) chervil
- 1 oz. (30 g) fresh tarragon
- 1 oz. (30 g) fresh cilantro
- $^{1}/_{3}$ oz. (10 g) fresh mint
- $^{1}/_{3}$ oz. (10 g) chives
- 3 $^{1}/_{2}$ oz. (100 g) low-fat or Greek-style yogurt
- Juice of 1 lemon
- Sea salt and freshly ground black pepper

Wash the salad and herb leaves. Cook them for about 3 minutes in boiling salted water then plunge them immediately into iced water.
Dry the herbs between sheets of paper towel to extract the water. Put the herbs, yogurt, and lemon juice into a food processor or blender and mix.
Season with salt and pepper.

Tip: Serve with salad or to accompany smoked fish or a tartare.

MANGO AND WHOLEGRAIN MUSTARD VINAIGRETTE

SERVES 8

PREPARATION TIME 5 MINUTES

- 3 tablespoons extra virgin olive oil
- 3 tablespoons sunflower oil
- 3 tablespoons walnut oil
- 3 tablespoons cider vinegar
- 3 tablespoons mango puree (available in cans, cartons, or frozen)
- 1 tablespoon wholegrain mustard
- 3–4 tablespoons water
- Sea salt and freshly ground black pepper

Put all the ingredients in a blender and blend for a few minutes, gradually adding the water until the dressing is of the desired consistency.

Tip: Serve to accompany salad, scampi, or fish.

VEGETABLE SAUCE

MAKES 4 1/4 CUPS (2 PINTS/1 LITER)

PREPARATION TIME 20 MINUTES

- 2 tablespoons wholegrain mustard
- 1 egg white
- 1 cup ($^{1}/_{2}$ pint/250 ml) pureed cooked vegetables (celeriac, carrots, pumpkin, zucchini)
- Juice of 2 lemons
- Scant $^{1}/_{2}$ cup (100 ml) extra virgin olive oil
- 2 cups (1 pint/500 ml) vegetable stock
- Selection of ground spices (cardamom, coriander, curry, cumin, star anise)
- Sea salt and freshly ground black pepper or long pepper

In a bowl, mix together the mustard and egg white. Add the vegetable puree, lemon juice, olive oil, and vegetable stock and mix until smooth. Add water if you want to thin the sauce.
Season to taste with salt, pepper, and the spices of your choice.

Tip: This is a very light sauce as some of the oil has been replaced by vegetables.

VEGETABLE STOCK

MAKES 8 $\frac{1}{2}$ CUPS (4 $\frac{1}{4}$ PINTS/2 LITERS)
PREPARATION TIME 1 HOUR

- 2 onions
- 4 cloves
- 8 $\frac{1}{2}$ cups (4 $\frac{1}{4}$ pints/2 liters) water
- 2 large carrots
- Green parts of 2 leeks
- 2 fennel stalks
- 2 white celery stalks, including leaves
- 2 green celery stalks, including leaves
- 4 thyme sprigs
- 2 bay leaves
- 2 juniper berries, crushed
- 10 parsley sprigs
- 1 tablespoon white peppercorns

Cut the onions in half and stick a clove in each half.
Coarsely chop the other vegetables.
Put all the ingredients in a pot, bring to a boil, then reduce the heat to just below simmering point and leave for
45 minutes. Let cool then pour through a sieve.

Tip: The wider the selection of vegetables used the better the stock will be.
You can also include leftover vegetables and trimmings.

PAGE 38: Fresh, steamed asparagus drizzled with olive oil and sprinkled with salt and pepper is a beautiful dish for the season.
PAGE 39: Every spring it's time to take out our collection of pottery, which we use throughout the season, as well as during summer. A mixture of French, Spanish, and Italian creations, good pottery offers a lifetime of versatile use in almost any setting.
RIGHT: A mix of vegetarian salads and hearty grains is ready to be served in the flower garden for lunch.

Above: Mentioned on many pages of this book and always close at hand in my kitchen, turmeric (curcuma) is a wonderful spice and an indispensable everyday ingredient. It adds a lovely color and flavor to many dishes and recipes.
Facing page: This vegetarian dish can be served on its own or accompanied by oven roasted fish (e.g., sardine, tuna, or swordfish).

ARUGULA AND GREEN AND YELLOW ZUCCHINI SALAD

SERVES 4 / PREPARATION TIME 15 MINUTES

- 10 $^1/_2$ oz. (300 g) arugula
- 1 yellow zucchini
- 1 green zucchini
- 7 or 8 tablespoons extra virgin olive oil
- 1 shallot, finely chopped
- 1 garlic clove, finely chopped
- 1 teaspoon cumin seeds
- 1 pinch of curry powder
- 1 teaspoon Dijon mustard
- 2 tablespoons lemon juice
- 1 teaspoon honey
- Sea salt and freshly ground black pepper

Cut each zucchini in quarters lengthwise. Remove the central part and cut the flesh into diamond shapes.
Heat 2 tablespoons of the oil in a frying pan and sweat the shallot and garlic. Add the pieces of zucchini and sauté but without browning. Add the cumin seeds and curry powder.
To make the dressing, mix together 5 or 6 tablespoons of olive oil, the mustard, lemon juice, honey, and salt and pepper. Put the arugula in a salad bowl with the warm zucchini, pour over the dressing, and toss.
Serve with broiled fish or as a starter with buffalo mozzarella or a carpaccio.

Tip: You could also add a few capers to this salad.

POACHED FENNEL WITH TURMERIC, SPICED RICOTTA, AND TOMATO SAUCE

SERVES 4

PREPARATION TIME 30 MINUTES

- 2 large fennel bulbs
- 4 $^1/_4$ cups (2 pints/1 liter) vegetable stock
- 1 tablespoon curry powder
- 1 tablespoon ground turmeric
For the spiced ricotta:
- 6 tablespoons (3 $^1/_2$ oz./100 g) ricotta
- $^1/_2$ teaspoon ground turmeric
- 1 teaspoon curry powder
- 4 fresh sage leaves, chopped
- Juice of $^1/_2$ lemon
- Sea salt and freshly ground black pepper
For the tomato sauce:
- 4 large tomatoes (approximately 2 lb. 3 oz./1 kg)
- Scant $^1/_4$ cup (50 ml) extra virgin olive oil
- 1 shallot, finely chopped
- 1 garlic clove, finely chopped
- 1 teaspoon ketchup
- 1 teaspoon wholegrain mustard

Preheat the oven to 350°F (180°C/gas 4). Trim the fennel bulbs and cook them for 15 to 20 minutes in the vegetable stock seasoned with the 1 tablespoon each of curry powder and ground turmeric. Meanwhile, make the spiced ricotta: put the ricotta in a bowl along with the ground turmeric, curry powder, chopped sage, lemon juice, and salt and pepper and mash together using a fork.
To make the tomato sauce, plunge the tomatoes into boiling water for 20 seconds. Let cool under running water, then peel off their skins and chop them coarsely. Heat the olive oil in a pan and add the chopped tomatoes, chopped shallot and garlic, ketchup, and wholegrain mustard. Cook over a medium heat, stirring occasionally, until the sauce has reduced. Cut the fennel bulbs in half lengthwise, place them in a roasting pan, and cover each with the spiced ricotta. Spoon over the tomato sauce. Cook in the preheated oven for 10 minutes.

At the Axel Vervoordt Company's offices at Kanaal, an employee lunch is served next to a bouquet of daisies. The menu includes a mixed green salad, eggplant salad with yogurt and cucumber dressing (see recipe on page 99), spiced celeriac chutney (see recipe on page 94), as well as a yellow and green zucchini curry with chives (see recipe on page 85). Having a luncheon together is about sharing and taking time out of the day to nourish the body. With Patrick's skill and supervision, we offer an employee lunch five days a week, where everyone is welcome to join their clients and colleagues to have a meal together. It's inspiring to see the conversations that everyone shares as it gives many people a chance to socialize and communicate, while offering a healthy, convenient option for lunch.

ZUCCHINI TARTLETS WITH CUMIN

Makes 20 tartlets
Preparation time 3 hours (including pastry resting time)

For the pastry:
- 2 cups (7 oz./200 g) all-purpose flour
- Pinch of salt
- 1 teaspoon ground cumin
- Pinch of sugar
- $^1/_2$ teaspoon dried yeast
- $^1/_2$ cup (120 ml) warm water
- $^1/_2$ tablespoon olive oil

For the filling:
- 1 zucchini, cut into julienne strips
- 1 tablespoon cumin seeds
- $^1/_4$ cup (3 $^1/_2$ oz./100 g) pesto (see recipe p. 77)
- 1 $^3/_4$ oz. (50 g) ricotta
- 1 $^3/_4$ oz. (50 g) feta (goat's or sheep's)

To make the pastry, sift the flour, salt, and cumin together into a bowl. Dissolve the sugar and yeast in the warm water. Place the seasoned flour and the sugar and yeast mixture into a food processor fitted with a hook. Add the olive oil and mix until you have a smooth, non-sticky pastry. Place the pastry in a bowl, cover with plastic wrap, and leave to rest in the fridge for 1 hour. Using a fork, or in a blender, mix together the pesto, ricotta, and feta. Keep at room temperature.

Remove the pastry from the fridge an hour before you want to use it. Preheat the oven to 350°F (180°C/gas 4). Using a rolling pin, roll out the pastry thinly and cut out 20 rounds to fit into the 3 in. (7.5 cm) holes of two 12-hole muffin pans. Press the pastry rounds gently into the pans. Put a layer of pesto and cheese mixture into the base of each pastry case, then top with a few strips of zucchini. Sprinkle each tartlet with the cumin seeds. Cook in the oven for 6–8 minutes.

Tip: You can make the cheese pesto in larger quantities and freeze it until required.

BULGUR WITH BABY CARROTS AND AYURVEDIC SPICES

SERVES 4

PREPARATION TIME 30 MINUTES

- 1 cup (7 oz./200 g) bulgur
- 1 bunch (about 1 lb. / 500 g) baby carrots, peeled and finely sliced
- 1 tablespoon mustard seeds
- 1 teaspoon cumin seeds
- 2 tablespoons extra virgin olive oil
- 1 large shallot, chopped
- 1 garlic clove, chopped
- 1 tablespoon chopped fresh gingerroot
- 1 kaffir lime leaf
- 1 teaspoon ground cinnamon
- 1 teaspoon ground cardamom
- 1 teaspoon ground turmeric
- 2 cups (1 pint/500 ml) vegetable stock
- Sea salt and freshly ground black pepper
- 1 lemon or scant $1/2$ cup (100 ml) cider vinegar
- 1 handful of cilantro leaves

In a skillet, dry-fry the mustard and cumin seeds. Add 1 tablespoon of olive oil and the chopped shallot and garlic, and let sweat for a few minutes.
Stir in the gingerroot, kaffir lime leaf, and ground cinnamon, cardamom, and turmeric. Pour in the bulgur and the vegetable stock. Cover and leave to cook over a low heat for 7 minutes.
Cook the carrot slices in boiling salted water for about 3 to 4 minutes, until al dente, then add the cooked carrots to the bulgur.
Season to taste with salt, pepper, the remaining olive oil, and lemon juice or cider vinegar.
Sprinkle with the cilantro leaves before serving.

Tip: For even more flavor, the carrots can be cooked in vegetable stock.

BRAISED SUCRINES

SERVES 4

PREPARATION TIME 20 MINUTES

- 2 sucrines
- 8 fresh mint leaves, chopped
- 1 small piece of butter or ghee
- 1 shallot, finely chopped
- 1 garlic clove, finely chopped
- Sea salt and freshly ground black pepper
- Scant 1 cup (200 ml) strong vegetable stock
- $1/4$ cup (60 ml) extra virgin olive oil
- Juice of 1 lemon

Wash and pat dry the sucrines, keeping them whole. Cut them in half lengthwise. Tuck the chopped mint between the leaves.
Melt the butter or ghee in a pan and sweat the shallot and garlic, then add the sucrines. Season with salt and pepper. Pour in the vegetable stock, cover the pan, and simmer over a low heat for 10 minutes.
Remove the sucrines from their cooking liquid and keep warm. Continue to simmer the cooking liquid until two-thirds has evaporated, then stir in the olive oil and lemon juice.
Place the sucrines in a serving dish and pour over the sauce.

Tip: You could also serve these sucrines with fresh peas or fava beans.

Note: Ghee is a clarified butter from the Indian subcontinent. It is obtained by simmering unsalted butter until all the water has evaporated. The fat floats to the surface and solidifies. This is the ghee, which is separated from solid particles, such as lactose. Ghee can be stored without refrigeration.

FACING PAGE: The azaleas bloom for several weeks in springtime and provide the perfect scenery and environment for an inspiring lunch table set for two, overlooking a small pond. In the basket are freshly picked nettles, alongside Nettle Soup, Frittata with Nettles and Lemon, and individual portions of Tomato Sauce (recipes on pages 48, 49, and 54 respectively).

ABOVE AND FACING PAGE: Nettles are wild herbs, known for their naturally detoxifying qualities. Containing useful vitamins and minerals that offer many benefits for the body, nettles are used as a treatment to help alleviate allergies, such as hay fever and inflammation. Its curative benefits make it an enduring spring favorite.

GREEN SALAD WITH MANGO AND GRILLED SWEET POTATO

SERVES 4
PREPARATION TIME 40 MINUTES

- 1 bunch (3 ½ oz./100 g) arugula
- 3 ½ oz. (100 g) lamb's lettuce
- 3 ½ oz. (100 g) heart of curly lettuce
- 2 sucrines
- 2 small sweet potatoes
- 1 mango, not too ripe
- ¼ cup (60 ml) extra virgin olive oil
- Sea salt and freshly ground black pepper
- Juice of 1 lemon

Cook the sweet potatoes in their skins in a pan of boiling water until al dente. Let cool, then peel and slice lengthwise. Heat a little olive oil in a skillet and brown the sweet potato slices. Season with salt, pepper, and a drizzle of lemon juice.
Peel the mango and cut into strips.
Trim, wash, and spin or pat dry the salad leaves.
In a salad bowl, mix together the salad leaves and sweet potato, then add the mango. Season with salt, pepper, lemon juice, and olive oil.

Tip: Serve with Mango and Wholegrain Mustard Vinaigrette (see p. 40). You could also add some toasted seeds (e.g., pumpkin, sunflower, pine nuts).

NETTLE SOUP

SERVES 8
PREPARATION TIME 1 HOUR

- 2 lb. 3 oz. (1 kg) young nettles (tops and leaves without the stalks)
- 1 small piece of butter
- 1 celery stalks, coarsely chopped
- 2 leeks, coarsely chopped
- 2 large white onions, coarsely chopped
- 2 garlic cloves, finely chopped
- 1 lemongrass stalk, finely chopped
- 2 kaffir lime leaves
- 1 untreated lemon
- 8 ½ cups (4 ¼ pints/2 liters) vegetable stock
- 10 flat-leaf parsley sprigs
- 7 oz. (200 g) chervil
- Sea salt and freshly ground black pepper

Wash the nettles and rinse them in plenty of water. Pat the leaves dry, set aside a few leaves for a garnish, then chop the remainder coarsely.
Melt the butter in a large pan and sweat the celery, leek, onion, garlic, lemongrass, kaffir lime leaves, and the zest of ½ lemon for 3–4 minutes.
Pour in the vegetable stock and simmer gently for 20 minutes.
Add the nettles, parsley, and chervil and cook for a further 5 minutes.
Puree the soup using a hand-held blender or in a food processor and, if you wish, strain it. Season with salt, pepper, and the juice of 1 lemon.
Finely chop the reserved nettle leaves and sprinkle over the soup to garnish.

Tip: It is advisable to wear gloves when harvesting and preparing the nettles.

Frittata with Nettles and Lemon

SERVES 12

PREPARATION TIME 1 HOUR

- 2 lb. 3 oz. (1 kg) young nettles (tops and leaves without the stalks)
- 10 ¹/₂ oz. (300 g) chervil
- 10 ¹/₂ oz. (300 g) spinach
- 1 small piece of butter
- 1 large onion, coarsely chopped
- 1 garlic clove, finely chopped
- 1 leek, coarsely chopped
- 1 head of celery, coarsely chopped
- 2 cups (1 pint/500 ml) vegetable stock
- 8 whole eggs plus 2 egg yolks
- Sea salt and freshly ground black pepper
- Juice of 2 lemons
- 1 puff pastry circle (8 oz./230 g—to fit an 11 in./28 cm pie plate)

Wash the nettles, chervil, and spinach and pat them dry. Chop them coarsely using a large knife.

Melt the butter in a large pan. Add the chopped onion, garlic, leek, and celery, and sweat. Pour in the stock and simmer for 20 minutes.

Then add the nettles, chervil, and spinach. Purée using a hand-held blender or in a food processor and, if you wish, strain the mixture. Let cool.

Meanwhile, preheat the oven to 325°F (160°C/gas 3).

Lightly beat the eggs using a fork and mix into the pureed vegetable mixture. Season with salt, pepper, and lemon juice. Line an 11 in. (28 cm) pie plate with parchment paper, then with the pastry. Prick the pastry all over using a fork. Pour the vegetable and egg mixture into it and cook in the oven for 30 minutes.

Tip: Serve with Yogurt and Fresh Herb Sauce (see p. 40) for a light and healthy lunch.

WHITE AND GREEN ASPARAGUS TIMBALES

SERVES 8

PREPARATION TIME 1 HOUR 20 MINUTES

- 1 bunch white asparagus
- 1 bunch green asparagus
- 1 small piece of butter
- 1 small onion, coarsely chopped
- 1 garlic clove, finely chopped
- 1 celery stalk, coarsely chopped
- 1 leek (white part only), coarsely chopped
- 2 cups (1 pint/500 ml) vegetable stock
- Scant cup (200 ml) soy cream
- 1 tablespoon chopped tarragon
- 3 tablespoons extra virgin olive oil
- Juice of $^1/_2$ lemon
- Sea salt, freshly ground long (or black) pepper, and freshly grated nutmeg
- 4 eggs, beaten

Peel the asparagus using a vegetable peeler. Cut about 4 in. (10 cm) of each stalk into small pieces, reserving the asparagus tips.

Heat the butter in a pan and brown the onion, garlic, celery, and leek. Add the chopped asparagus stalks, vegetable stock, soy cream, and chopped tarragon and simmer for 20 minutes.

Puree the soup using a hand-held blender or in a food processor, then strain (optional). Let cool.

Meanwhile, preheat the oven to 325°F (160°C/gas 3) and cook the asparagus tips in boiling salted water for about 8–10 minutes, until al dente.

Slice them diagonally.

Combine the olive oil and lemon juice and season with salt, pepper, and nutmeg. Pour the mixture over the asparagus tips and keep warm.

Mix the eggs into the thick soup and pour into 8 ramekins. Cook in a bain-marie (hot water bath) in the oven for 30 to 45 minutes.

Remove the ramekins from the oven and arrange the cooked asparagus tips on top of each one.

Pizza with Roasted Tomatoes and Thai Basil

SERVES 12

PREPARATION TIME 2 HOURS (PLUS 2 HOURS
RESTING TIME FOR THE PIZZA DOUGH)

For the pizza dough:
- 2 tablespoons (1 oz./25 g) unsalted butter
- 2 tablespoons (30 ml) extra virgin olive oil
- 1 oz. (30 g) fresh yeast or 2 teaspoons active dried yeast
- 5 cups (1 lb./500 g) all-purpose flour
- 1 teaspoon dried oregano
- 2 teaspoons sea salt
- 1 cup (¹/₂ pint/250 ml) warm water

For the roasted tomatoes:
- 2 shallots, finely chopped
- 2 garlic cloves, finely chopped
- Leaves from 8 Thai basil sprigs, finely chopped
- 2 tablespoons ketchup
- Scant ¹/₂ cup (100 ml) extra virgin olive oil (plus extra for drizzling)
- Sea salt and freshly ground black pepper
- 2 lb. 3 oz. (1 kg) cherry vine tomatoes, cut in half

For the ricotta:
- 1 lb. (500 g) ricotta
- 1 lemon
- Sea salt and freshly ground black pepper

To make the pizza dough, melt the butter in a small frying pan, add the olive oil, and mix the yeast into the warm fats. In a large bowl, mix together the flour, dried oregano, and salt. Pour over the oil mixture, add 1 cup (¹/₂ pint/250 ml) warm water, and knead to form a smooth dough. Chill for 1 hour, then move the bowl to a warm place and let rest for a further 1 hour.

To make the roasted tomatoes, preheat the oven to 250°F (120°C/gas 1/2). In a bowl, mix together the shallots, garlic, half the chopped basil, ketchup, olive oil, salt and pepper. Add the tomatoes and stir to coat them in the mixture. Arrange the tomatoes in a roasting pan and cook in the oven for 1 hour. Remove the tomatoes from the oven and increase

the oven temperature to 350°F (180°C/gas 4).

To make the pizza, spread the dough out on a baking sheet to form a rectangle ¹/₈ in. (3 mm) thick.

In a bowl, mash the ricotta with the zest from half the lemon and all the juice and season to taste. Spread this ricotta mixture over the pizza dough, arrange the tomatoes over the top, and bake the pizza in the oven for 20 minutes. Before serving, scatter the remaining chopped basil over the pizza and drizzle with olive oil.

Avocado Salad with Zucchini and Red Chili Pepper

SERVES 4

PREPARATION TIME 20 MINUTES

- 1 yellow zucchini
- 1 green zucchini
- 2 ripe avocados
- About 2 tablespoons olive oil for sautéing

For the dressing:
- ¹/₂ teaspoon cumin seeds
- ¹/₂ cup extra virgin olive oil
- Juice of 1 lemon
- 1 red chili pepper, seeded and finely sliced
- 1 teaspoon wholegrain mustard
- Leaves from 6 cilantro sprigs, finely chopped
- 1 teaspoon honey
- Sea salt and freshly ground black pepper

To make the dressing, dry-fry the cumin seeds in a small frying pan. Put them in a bowl with the olive oil, lemon juice, chili, mustard, and cilantro and mix together. Stir in the honey and season with salt and pepper.

Slice the zucchini into ¹/₈ in. (3 mm) slices and sauté in a little olive oil. Peel the avocado and slice it lengthwise into 10 slices.

Put the zucchini and avocado slices in a salad bowl, pour over the dressing, and toss gently, being careful to avoid breaking the avocado slices.

PAGES 50–51: On a table in front of the windows in the orangery, a collection of side dishes for a luncheon with several friends is ready to be served. The platter in the rear is filled with sautéed zucchini tossed with a mixture of herbs. In the front, a fresh tomato salad with capers and cilantro sits next to grilled eggplant.

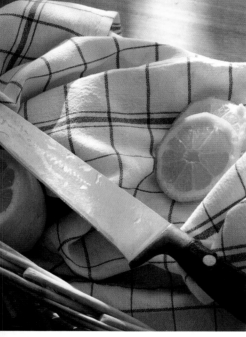

ABOVE: For anyone who spends time in the kitchen, the importance of lemons cannot be underestimated. We always have lemons in our home. In the kitchen, their natural acidity adds freshness, which helps release the taste of many dishes. In the home, lemons are inherently decorative and add a burst of color to a room.

EGGPLANT, FENNEL, AND TOMATO GRATIN

SERVES 4

PREPARATION TIME 75 MINUTES

For the eggplant puree
- 2 eggplants
- 4 tablespoons extra virgin olive oil
- 1 large shallot, finely chopped
- 1 garlic clove, finely chopped
- 6 tablespoons soy sauce
- $^1/_2$ lemon
- Leaves of 1 thyme sprig
- Freshly ground black pepper

For the poached fennel with turmeric
- 2 medium fennel bulbs
- 2 cups (1 pint/500 ml) vegetable stock
- 1 teaspoon ground turmeric
- 1 teaspoon Madras curry powder
- Sea salt and freshly ground black pepper

For the tomato sauce
- 1 small piece of butter
- 1 shallot, finely chopped
- 1 garlic clove, finely chopped
- 1 teaspoon wholegrain mustard
- 1 tablespoon ketchup
- 4 ripe tomatoes, peeled and diced (see tip)
- 8 large basil leaves, chopped
- Sea salt and freshly ground black pepper

To make the eggplant puree, preheat the oven to 350°F (180°C/gas 4). Cut the eggplants in half lengthwise and put in a roasting pan, skin side down. Using a paring knife, score crosses in the flesh, without cutting through the skin. Sprinkle with 3 tablespoons of the olive oil and the thyme and cook in the oven for 10 minutes before removing.
Heat the remaining 1 tablespoon of olive oil in a pan and sweat the shallot and garlic until transparent.
When the eggplants are cooked, remove the flesh (see Tip), then dice it, and mix with the soy sauce. Stir into the shallots and garlic and cook for a further few minutes over a medium heat.
Season to taste with pepper and lemon juice.

Meanwhile, to make the poached fennel, remove any remaining stems and the tough outer leaves from the fennel bulbs, then cut them in half vertically.
Put the stock, turmeric, curry powder, and salt and pepper into a pan, add the fennel, and cook for about 12 minutes until al dente. Remove from the pan and slice into thin ($^1/_8$ in./3 mm) strips.
For the tomato sauce, heat the butter in a pan and sweat the shallot, and garlic. Stir in the mustard and ketchup, then add the peeled, diced tomatoes and cook over a medium heat, uncovered, until nearly all the liquid has evaporated. Sprinkle in the chopped basil and season with salt and pepper before serving.

Assembling the dish. Preheat the oven to 325°F (160°C/gas 3). Mix the eggplant and the fennel in a gratin dish. Cover with the tomato sauce and bake in the oven for 20 minutes.

Tip: The easiest way to remove the flesh from the cooked half eggplants is to use a soup spoon.
The fennel trimmings can be used in a stock.
To peel tomatoes (and fruit with thin skins such as peaches), plunge them into boiling water for 30 seconds, then into cold water. The skin will then easily slip away from the flesh.

> " THE FOOD SHE SERVES IS ALWAYS
> DELICIOUS YET HEALTHY. HER INGREDIENTS
> REFLECT AND RESPECT THE SEASON AND,
> FOR THE MOST PART, ARRIVE ON YOUR PLATE
> STRAIGHT FROM HER VEGETABLE GARDEN.
>
> *Dries Van Noten*

FACING PAGE: A geranium variety provides a pleasant setting for a table often used for outdoor lunches and afternoon tea. The close connection I feel to nature is one that is developed every day from spending as much time outside as possible to appreciate its splendor. A short walk away from this table, we have a space in our garden where we keep several chickens. One breed of chicken we have is known as an Araucana chicken, a special type of bird that's said to originate from Chile and is famous for laying blue-shelled eggs. Often when friends visit for breakfast and we serve blue eggs, they ask if we've specially decorated the eggs for the occasion. After a tour of the garden, friends are always surprised when they get to see in person the unique chickens and their beautifully blue-colored eggs.

CHICKEN COATED WITH SESAME SEEDS AND TARRAGON

SERVES 4

PREPARATION TIME: 20 MINUTES

- 2 free-range chicken fillets (preferably black leg or Bresse)
- 3 $^1/_2$ oz. (100 g) sesame seeds
- $^1/_2$ teaspoon ground cumin
- $^1/_2$ teaspoon ground coriander
- $^1/_2$ teaspoon ground fenugreek
- $^1/_3$ cup (1 $^3/_4$ oz./50 g) grated Parmesan
- Leaves from 3 tarragon sprigs, chopped
- Sea salt and freshly ground black pepper
- 1 garlic clove, finely chopped
- 3 egg whites, lightly beaten
- $^1/_4$ cup (60 ml) extra virgin olive oil
- $^1/_4$ lemon and a few extra tarragon leaves, to serve

In a frying pan, lightly dry-fry the sesame seeds, cumin, coriander, and fenugreek. Let cool, transfer to a plate, and stir in the grated Parmesan and half the chopped tarragon.

Cut the chicken fillets into $^1/_4$-in ($^1/_2$-cm) thick strips.

On a plate, mix together the salt, pepper, garlic, and the remaining chopped tarragon. Dip each of the chicken strips into this mixture.

Dip each of the chicken strips into the beaten egg whites, then into the spice and Parmesan mix, ensuring that they are lightly coated all over.

Heat the olive oil in a skillet and fry the chicken strips gently until the coating is golden and crispy.

To serve, squeeze over some lemon juice and sprinkle with tarragon leaves.

Tip: You can also serve these chicken strips as an hors-d'oeuvre, with soy sauce or a horseradish or wasabi dressing.

SALMON SASHIMI WITH SOY SAUCE AND SESAME SEEDS

SERVES 4

PREPARATION TIME 20 MINUTES

- 9 oz. (250 g) salmon fillet (1 in./2.5 cm thick)
- Sea salt and freshly ground black pepper
- Scant $^1/_2$ cup (100 ml) soy sauce
- Scant $^1/_4$ cup (50 ml) extra virgin olive oil
- Juice of 1/2 lemon
- $^1/_4$ teaspoon wasabi paste
- 3 tablespoons black sesame seeds
- 3 tablespoons white sesame seeds
- $^1/_2$ teaspoon ground coriander
- $^1/_2$ teaspoon ground cardamom

Season the salmon with salt and pepper. In a small bowl, mix together the soy sauce, olive oil, lemon juice, and wasabi paste.

Put the salmon in a dish, pour over the marinade, and turn the fish to coat. Let marinate 5 minutes.

In a skillet, dry-fry the sesame seeds and ground coriander and cardamom. Remove from the heat and let cool. Remove the salmon from the marinade and coat in the spice mixture.

Heat a frying pan over a high heat and sear the salmon on both sides. Remove from the heat, let cool, then put it in the freezer for 10 minutes to make it easier to cut.

Slice the salmon thinly and arrange on a serving dish.

Tip: Serve with a bulgur wheat or fresh herb salad.

SLOW-COOKED EGGPLANT WITH SOY SAUCE

SERVES 8

PREPARATION TIME 40 MINUTES

- Scant 1 cup (200 ml) vegetable or chicken stock
- 1 tablespoon extra virgin olive oil
- 4 tablespoons soy sauce
- 4 eggplants
- Sea salt and freshly ground black pepper
- 1 garlic clove, finely chopped
- $^1/_2$ lemon

In a bowl, mix together the stock, olive oil, and soy sauce.

Cut the eggplants in half lengthwise, then, using a paring knife, score the flesh, making several crosses.

Place the eggplants in a large pan, flesh side up. Pour over the stock mixture, season with salt and pepper, and sprinkle with the chopped garlic. Cook over a low heat for about 30 minutes, turning the eggplants every 2 or 3 minutes, until nearly all the liquid has evaporated. Adjust seasoning as necessary, drizzle with lemon juice, and serve.

Tip: Serve these eggplants as a vegetarian meal, as a salad with Yogurt and Fresh Herb Sauce (see p. 40), or diced as a vegetarian tartare.

ABOVE, TOP: A selection of flowering branches from a *Kalmia latifolia* plant adds a welcome color and texture to an entrance hall.

ABOVE, BOTTOM: Slow-cooked eggplant served on a rustic, wooden plate is a nice reminder to choose serving dishes that will harmonize well with the courses they will be used for.

> " MAY'S CUISINE IS A BLEND OF
SIMPLICITY, THE FINEST PRODUCE,
AND GREAT STYLISHNESS. THERE'S
ALWAYS MORE TO DISCOVER BECAUSE
SHE'S ALWAYS TRYING OUT NEW IDEAS.
>
> *Katia Labèque*

PAGES 60–61: A lunch buffet is served on a long table in the shade of wisteria overlooking a small pond. Especially when presenting buffet options, I always consciously try to offer food combinations that avoid a mix of proteins—such as not serving fish and meat as part of the same meal—to help aid healthy digestion. The best part about buffet service is being able to share the experience of a meal with more friends. The act of passing food and offering additional portions is an interactive and timeless gesture that demonstrates care for every guest.
BELOW: A blue and white luncheon served under a natural awning.

CHICKPEA, TOMATO, AND CORIANDER CASSEROLE

SERVES 4

PREPARATION 45 MINUTES, PLUS SOAKING OVERNIGHT

- $^1/_2$ cup (5 oz./140 g) dried chickpeas
- 4 large tomatoes (about 2 lb. 3 oz./1 kg)
- 1 teaspoon coriander seeds
- 1 teaspoon cumin seeds
- 1 teaspoon white mustard seeds
- 4–6 tablespoons extra virgin olive oil
- 2 shallots, finely chopped
- 2 garlic cloves, finely chopped
- 1 teaspoon red curry paste
- Scant 1 cup (200 ml) coconut milk
- Scant 1 cup (200 ml) passata (sieved tomato pulp)
- 1 teaspoon ground paprika
- $^1/_2$ teaspoon ground cinnamon
- $^1/_2$ teaspoon Madras curry powder
- Sea salt and freshly ground black pepper
- Leaves of 10 cilantro sprigs, chopped

Put the dried chickpeas in a bowl, cover with cold water, and leave to soak overnight in the fridge. The following day, rinse them well.

In a skillet, dry-fry the coriander, cumin, and mustard seeds until golden. Add the olive oil and sweat the shallots and onion. Stir in the curry paste, then add the chickpeas, coconut milk, passata, paprika, cinnamon, and curry powder and stir to combine.

Simmer, covered, over a low heat for 30 minutes, stirring regularly.

Meanwhile, peel the tomatoes (see Tip p. 54) and dice them into $^1/_2$ in. (1 cm) pieces.

Add to the chickpeas and continue to simmer for a further 5 minutes.

Season to taste with salt and pepper and sprinkle with the chopped cilantro just before serving.

ROASTED COD FILLET WITH LEMON AND SAGE

SERVES 4
PREPARATION TIME 20 MINUTES

- 1 lb. 12 oz. (800 g) skinless cod fillet
- 1 tablespoon coriander seeds
- Sea salt and freshly ground black pepper
- $\frac{1}{4}$ cup (60 ml) extra virgin olive oil
- 2 untreated lemons
- 8 large sage leaves, finely chopped

Preheat the oven to 350°F (180°C/gas 4). In a small skillet, dry-fry the coriander seeds until they release their aroma, then crush them in a mortar using a pestle. Season the cod with salt, pepper, and the crushed coriander.
Lightly oil a roasting pan and put the fish into it.
Peel and remove all the pith from 1 lemon (see Tip p. 28) and cut the flesh into half-moons.
Drizzle the olive oil and the juice of the remaining lemon over the fish, then sprinkle with the chopped sage.
Cook in the oven for 10 minutes. Serve on a large serving dish, with the cooking juices poured over the top.

Tip: Serve the cod with steamed vegetables and rice.

AYURVEDIC-STYLE SEA BASS FILLET

SERVES 4
PREPARATION TIME 30 MINUTES

- 1 lb. 12 oz. (800 g) skinless sea bass fillet
- $\frac{1}{4}$ cup (1 oz./30 g) coriander seeds
- 1 teaspoon cumin seeds
- 1 teaspoon black mustard seeds
- $\frac{1}{4}$ cup (60 ml) extra virgin olive oil
- Juice of 1 lemon
- Sea salt and freshly ground black pepper
For the ayurvedic mixture:
- 1 garlic clove
- 1 oz. (30 g) galangal root
- 1 oz. (30 g) fresh gingerroot
- 1 oz. (30 g) lemongrass stalk
- 2 kaffir lime leaves
- 4 dried sage leaves

Preheat the oven to 325°F (160°C/gas 3). In a hot skillet, dry-fry the coriander, cumin, and mustard seeds. As soon as they begin to release their aromas, remove them from the heat and spread them out on a plate to stop them cooking further.
Using a paring knife, peel the garlic, galangal, gingerroot, and lemongrass. Chop them coarsely then put them in a food processor with the dry-fried seeds, kaffir lime leaves, and sage leaves and chop finely.
Put the sea bass fillet into a roasting pan. Season with salt and pepper. Drizzle with olive oil and lemon juice. Spread the ayurvedic mixture evenly over the fish. Place into the preheated oven and bake for 15 minutes.

Tip: You can prepare a larger quantity of the ayuvedic mixture and freeze portions.

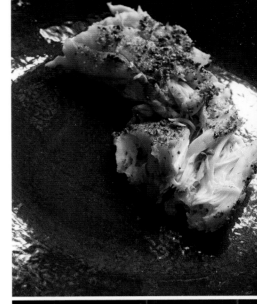

ABOVE, BOTTOM: A view of the kitchen cupboard in Venice filled with white porcelain, ideal for use when serving a large number of guests. A colorful bowl of tomato salsa sits next to hearty lentils. These are easy dishes to make and can be served as healthy starters. They also combine superbly with grilled fish.

POACHED EGGS WITH HOP SHOOTS

SERVES 4
PREPARATION TIME 20 MINUTES

- 4 fresh eggs
- 8 $^1/_2$ oz. (240 g) hop shoots
- 1 lemon
- 1 cup ($^1/_2$ pint/250 ml) soy cream
- Pinch of Madras curry powder
- Sea salt and freshly ground black pepper
- Scant $^1/_2$ cup (100 ml) white wine or alcohol vinegar

Trim the hop shoots, removing the lower hard part. Wash and dry them.
Cook them for about 3 minutes until al dente in 8 $^1/_2$ cups (4 $^1/_4$ pints/2 liters) of boiling water with the juice of $^1/_2$ the lemon.
Put the soy cream in a heavy-bottomed pan, stir in the curry powder, and heat until reduced by half.
Add the hop shoots, the juice of the remaining $^1/_2$ lemon, salt, and pepper. Keep warm.
Put 8 $^1/_2$ cups (4 $^1/_4$ pints/2 liters) of water and the vinegar in a pan and bring to a boil. Form a spiral in the center by drawing circles in the water with a whisk. Break one of the eggs into the center of this spiral and poach for 2–3 minutes until the white has completely set.
Repeat with the other eggs, poaching one at a time.
Divide the hop shoots evenly between four plates and place a poached egg on top of each one.

Tip: You can replace the hop shoots with bean sprouts if you wish.

ABOVE: The blue and white dining room offers nice light throughout the day and is the preferred setting for many breakfasts and lunches in our home.
FACING PAGE: A little-known delicacy, *jets de houblon* (hop shoots) are a delicious plant that grow on the French and Belgian border and are only harvested during a very fast, but very short, growing season, lasting only a few weeks each year. Crisp in taste and white in color, hop shoots have an earthy flavor, similar to bean sprouts or white asparagus.

GRILLED VEGETABLES WITH LEMON OIL

SERVES 4

PREPARATION TIME 20 MINUTES

- 1 yellow zucchini
- 1 green zucchini
- 8–9 tablespoons extra virgin olive oil
- 1 small shallot, finely chopped
- 1 garlic clove, finely chopped
- 8 basil leaves, finely chopped

For the dressing:
- Juice plus 1 teaspoon zest of 1 untreated lemon or lime
- $^1/_3$ cup (80 ml) extra virgin olive oil
- $^1/_2$ teaspoon Dijon mustard
- $^1/_2$ teaspoon honey
- Sea salt and freshly ground black pepper

Slice the zucchini thinly and put it in a bowl. Add 6 tablespoons of olive oil and stir to mix. Place them under a broiler or on a grill.

Heat 2–3 tablespoons of oil in a skillet and sweat the shallot and onion. Then add the zucchini. Season with salt and pepper and sprinkle with the chopped basil.

To make the dressing, put all the ingredients in a blender or food processor and mix.

Serve hot or warm, accompanied by the dressing, served separately in a bowl or jug.

Tip: If you prefer, you can replace the sauce with fresh ricotta mixed with lemon juice and basil.

PEA SOUP WITH EXTRA VIRGIN OLIVE OIL

SERVES 4

PREPARATION TIME 30 MINUTES

- 1 $^1/_3$ cups (7 oz./200 g) fresh or frozen peas
- Green part of 1 leek
- 2 green celery stalks
- 2 onions
- $^1/_4$ cup extra virgin olive oil
- 1 garlic clove, finely chopped
- 2 cups (1 pint/500 ml) vegetable stock
- 1 cardamom pod, crushed
- 10 fresh mint leaves, chopped
- Sea salt and freshly ground black pepper

Wash the leek and celery. Coarsely chop the leek, celery, and onions into equal-size pieces.

Heat the oil in a pan and sweat the leek, celery, onion, and garlic.

Add the vegetable stock and the crushed cardamom pod.

Simmer for 15 minutes, then add the peas and chopped mint.

Simmer for a further 5 minutes, then puree using a hand-held blender or in a food processor. Season with salt and pepper.

Strain the soup if you want a smoother consistency.

Divide between 4 soup plates and drizzle olive oil over each serving.

ABOVE, TOP: This recipe for pea soup can also be used as a vegetarian sauce to accompany vegetables. Simply reduce the quantity of stock by half.
FACING PAGE: For other tasty options with grilled vegetables, add a spoon of ricotta mixed with a bit of lemon and basil, or toss with vinaigrette.

RHUBARB TIRAMISU

SERVES 4

PREPARATION TIME 30 MINUTES (PLUS
RESTING TIME)

- 4 large rhubarb stalks
- 1 orange
- Scant 1 cup (200 ml) water
- Scant 1 cup (200 ml) red berry juice (ideally redcurrant)
- 2 tablespoons palm sugar
- Scant $^1/_2$ cup (100 ml) agave syrup
- 2 star anise
- 1 cinnamon stick
- 1 vanilla pod, broken in half lengthwise
- 1 teaspoon coriander seeds
- 3 egg yolks
- 3 tablespoons superfine granulated sugar
- 2 egg whites
- 1 $^1/_2$ cups (12 oz./350 g) mascarpone

Peel the orange, remove all the pith, and cut the flesh into small pieces. Put into a pan with the water, fruit juice, palm sugar, agave syrup, star anise, cinnamon stick, vanilla pod, and coriander seeds. Bring to a boil, then reduce the heat and simmer for 10 minutes.

Meanwhile, peel and trim the rhubarb stalks, then cut them into 2 in. (5 cm) lengths. Add to the syrup and cook over a medium heat for a further 5 minutes. Let cool in the syrup for 4–5 hours in the fridge.

To make the tiramisu, in a large bowl, whisk the egg yolks with half the sugar until the mixture reaches ribbon stage. In a separate bowl, whisk the egg whites until stiff, adding the remainder of the sugar toward the end of whisking. Stir the mascarpone into the beaten egg yolks, then, gently fold in the egg whites. Drain the rhubarb, reserving the juice for use elsewhere. Cover the bottom of a serving dish with a layer of rhubarb. Spoon a layer of the tiramisu on top.

Repeat these layers, finishing with a final layer of rhubarb.
Let rest for 3–4 hours in the fridge.

Tip: You could put the finishing touch on this dessert by sprinkling it with toasted slivered almonds and ground cinnamon or even ground aniseed.

COCONUT COOKIES

MAKES 20 COOKIES
PREPARATION TIME 15 MINUTES

- 1 ¹/₃ cups (3 ¹/₂ oz./100 g) shredded coconut
- Generous ¹/₃ cup (2 ¹/₂ oz./75 g) palm sugar
- 1 ¹/₂ tablespoons (³/₄ oz./20 g) unsalted butter, melted
- 1 whole egg plus 1 egg yolk

Preheat the oven to 350°F (180°C/gas 4). In a bowl, mix all the ingredients together to form a smooth dough.
Line a baking sheet with bakery paper. Drop spoonfuls of the mixture onto the baking sheet, spacing them evenly apart. Using a fork, spread them out to form flat rounds.
Cook in the oven until golden (about 10 to 20 minutes).

Tip: Before cooking, you could sprinkle the cookies with chopped pistachios or walnuts.

PISTACHIO COOKIES

MAKES 30 COOKIES
PREPARATION TIME 15 MINUTES

- 1 cup (3 ¹/₂ oz./100 g) pastry flour
- 1 cup (3 ¹/₂ oz./100 g) superfine granulated sugar
- Scant stick (3 ¹/₂ oz./100 g) unsalted butter, melted
- ²/₃ cup (150 ml) egg white (4–5 medium eggs)
- 2 tablespoons chopped pistachios

Preheat the oven to 350°F (180°C/gas 4). Using a spatula, mix the flour and sugar together in a bowl. Mix in the melted butter and then the egg whites (unbeaten).
Line a baking sheet with baking paper. Drop spoonfuls of the mixture onto the baking sheet and spread them out to form circles.
Sprinkle with the chopped pistachios then bake in the oven until golden (about 10 to 20 minutes).
Remove the cookies from the oven and let cool on a cooling rack.

Tip: Try sandwiching several of these cookies together with layers of white chocolate mousse.

SUMMER

Nature's abundant gifts shine throughout the garden with generous offerings of fruits and vegetables, each delivering delightful tastes and textures. From the light and airy qualities of leafy salads and greens, to the fresh flavors of tomatoes and sweet goodness of strawberries, each product helps inspire the menu while offering style to the table. When the flower gardens are in full bloom, we like to take long walks to enjoy the beautiful scents and colors. I fill my days with ephemeral tasks, such as collecting flowers and a variety of herbs and basil for grilled fish and salads. Whatever I don't find in the garden, the local markets can offer me guidance. Look for fruits and vegetables that add versatility, such as fruits that can be served as compote for breakfast and placed around the home and table throughout the day. Choose an intimate setting, indoors or outdoors, that offers an inspiring view, so that nature's beauty stimulates the conversation and the senses.

FACING PAGE: A bright summer table is set for several friends with yellow Provençal pottery and zinnia bouquets.
RIGHT: Ricotta crackers with cheese pâté and roasted vine tomatoes make a delicious appetizer that can be prepared in advance (see recipe on page 77).
PAGES 74–75: A collection of vegetables, including zucchini varieties and carrots, are harvested in the morning to prepare for an afternoon luncheon.

SESAME CARROT BALLS WITH CARROT PUREE

SERVES 12

PREPARATION TIME 40 MINUTES (PLUS 1 HOUR REFRIGERATION)

- 3 $\frac{1}{2}$ oz. (100 g) carrots, grated
- 7 oz. (200 g) mashed potato
- 2 tablespoons extra virgin olive oil
- 1 large shallot, finely chopped
- 2 garlic cloves, finely chopped
- 1 tablespoon toasted coriander seeds
- 1 tablespoon finely chopped fresh gingerroot
- 6 tablespoons mixed black and white sesame seeds, toasted

For the carrot puree:
- 7 oz. (200 g) carrots, peeled and sliced
- Scant $\frac{1}{4}$ cup (50 ml) virgin sesame oil
- Sea salt and freshly ground black pepper
- Scant 1 cup (200 ml) vegetable stock

Preheat the oven to 350°F (180°C/gas 4). Heat the olive oil in a skillet and sweat the shallot and garlic with the coriander seeds. Add the gingerroot and 2 tablespoons of the sesame seeds. Sweat for a further few minutes then let cool. Mix in the grated carrots and the potato puree and form small balls about $\frac{3}{4}$ in. (2 cm) in diameter. Refrigerate for at least an hour so that they are firm.

Meanwhile make the carrot puree, heat the sesame oil in a pan and sweat the carrot slices. Add salt and pepper, pour over the stock, and simmer gently, uncovered, until the liquid has evaporated.

Puree using a hand-held blender or in a food processor. Adjust the seasoning to taste.

Spread out the remaining 4 tablespoons of sesame seeds on a plate and roll the carrot balls in them until each is thoroughly coated. Warm them in the oven for 3 minutes.

Serve warm or cold in spoons with the carrot puree.

(Recipe photo on page 79.)

PESTO AND SESAME SEED STICKS

SERVES 4

PREPARATION TIME 15 MINUTES

- 1 tablespoon toasted sesame seeds
- 1 sheet of tortilla dough
- 10 large basil leaves
- 4 fresh mint leaves
- 1 tablespoon pine nuts
- 1 tablespoon grated Parmesan
- Zest of $1/2$ lemon
- $1/4$ cup (60 ml) extra virgin olive oil
- Sea salt and freshly ground black pepper

Preheat the oven to 300°F (150°C/gas 2). Line a baking sheet with baking paper, then with the tortilla dough.
In a food processor or blender, puree the basil, mint, pine nuts, Parmesan, lemon zest, olive oil, salt, and pepper.
Spread this pesto evenly over the dough, then sprinkle with the toasted sesame seeds.
Cut the dough into thin strips, each about $1/4$ in. ($1/2$ cm) wide and 10 in. (25 cm) long. Bake in the oven for 10 minutes.

Tip: You could replace the basil with arugula or use a mixture of the two.

RICOTTA CRACKERS WITH CHEESE PÂTÉ AND ROASTED VINE TOMATOES

SERVES 20

PREPARATION TIME 1 HOUR

- 40 crackers or toasted bruschetta
- 20 cherry vine tomatoes, cut in half
- Sea salt and freshly ground black pepper
- $1/4$ cup (4 tablespoons / 60 ml) extra virgin olive oil
- 1 teaspoon ketchup
- Leaves from $1/4$ bunch basil, chopped

For the cheese pâté:
- 1 garlic clove, finely chopped
- 1 shallot, finely chopped
- 1 $3/4$ oz. (50 g) feta cheese, crumbled
- 6 rounded tablespoons (3 $1/2$ oz./100 g) ricotta
- $1/4$ cup (1 $3/4$ oz./50 g) grated Parmesan
- 3 $1/2$ oz. (100 g) pesto (see recipe on left)
- Juice of $1/4$ lemon

Preheat the oven to 250°F (120°C/gas 1/2). Put the tomatoes in a roasting pan and season with salt and pepper.
In a small bowl, mix together 3 tablespoons of olive oil, ketchup, and chopped basil. Drizzle over the tomatoes and transfer to the oven for 50 minutes. Meanwhile, heat the remaining oil in a small frying pan and sweat the garlic and shallot for 3–4 minutes.
To make the cheese pâté, put the garlic, shallot, feta, ricotta, Parmesan, and pesto into a bowl and mash together with a fork. Season with the lemon juice and salt and pepper and stir well to combine. Spread some cheese pâté on each cracker and top with half a tomato.

Tip: You can substitute the roasted vine tomatoes with dried tomatoes or chopped fresh tomatoes drizzled with olive oil and seasoned with salt and pepper.

FACING PAGE: In summer, we often spend a lot of time in Venice, and while we're there we organize events, both big and small, for many friends from around the world. Here a large buffet is ready to be served in the courtyard of Palazzo Alvera.
ABOVE, TOP: Homemade pesto and sesame seed sticks are an ideal way to add a personal touch to any occasion. They only take around fifteen minutes to prepare, so you can make a lot in advance, and we even store them in metal boxes for use at a later date.

> **"** HER PHILOSOPHY REGARDING HEALTHY MEALS IS APPLIED TO EVERYTHING SHE DOES. THE PRESENTATION IS ALWAYS BREATHTAKING.
>
> *Melinda Blinken*

FACING PAGE: An inviting appetizer, carrot balls rolled in sesame seeds are served on a large platter with individual portions prepared on silver spoons (see recipe on page 76). It's important to use imagination in the kitchen when selecting a menu and presenting friends and guests with appetizer options. Finger foods should be as elegant in appearance as they are to taste. Patrick and I often serve vegetarian dishes as starters as they provide a nice complement to either fish or meat courses during the main meal, while offering balanced food combinations. If certain main courses are popular with guests, consider offering a mini-version as an appetizer in the future, such as smaller portions of poached fennel with turmeric, spiced ricotta, and tomato sauce (see recipe on page 42), or bite-sized grilled eggplant with soy sauce (see recipe on page 59).

TUNA CARPACCIO WITH OLIVES AND CAPERS

SERVES 4

PREPARATION TIME 20 MINUTES

- 5 tablespoons extra-virgin olive oil
- 7 oz. (200 g) yellowfin tuna (1 in./2.5 cm thick)
- Sea salt and freshly ground black pepper
- Juice of $1/2$ lemon
- 12 pitted black olives, sliced
- 12 pitted green olives, sliced
- 16 capers, crushed
- Leaves of 6 fresh cilantro sprigs, chopped
- $1/2$ teaspoon coriander seeds

Heat 1 tablespoon of the olive oil in a frying pan and sear the tuna. Let cool. Put the tuna in the freezer for 15 minutes to make it easier to slice.
Cut the cold tuna in very thin slices. Arrange them on a serving dish and season with salt, pepper, the remaining olive oil and the lemon juice.
In a small bowl, mix together the sliced olives, crushed capers, chopped cilantro, and coriander seeds. Sprinkle this mixture over the tuna slices.

Tip: Serve with very thin slices of toasted sourdough bread.

PAGES 80–81: A salad of black radish, turnip, and celeriac is served on a round, wooden tray (see recipe on this page). Very rich in vitamin C and fiber, the black radish is an ancient vegetable that was first cultivated in Egypt thousands of years ago.

BLACK RADISH, TURNIP, AND CELERIAC SALAD

SERVES 8

PREPARATION TIME 30 MINUTES

- 4 white turnips
- 1 small black radish
- 1 small celeriac
- 3 ½ oz. (100 g) snow peas
- 2 tablespoons chopped fresh horseradish
- 1 teaspoon Dijon mustard
- ⅓ cup (80 ml) sour cream
- Juice of 1 lemon
- Sea salt and freshly ground black pepper
- ¼ cup extra virgin olive oil
- 1 shallot, finely chopped
- 1 garlic clove, finely chopped

Peel the turnips, radish, and celeriac and cut them into julienne strips about 2 ½ in. (6 cm) long.
Julienne the snow peas.
Blanch all these vegetables for 1 minute in boiling salted water, then plunge them into iced water.
Drain the vegetables and put them in a salad bowl.
To make the dressing, mix the chopped horseradish and mustard into the sour cream. Add the lemon juice and season with salt and pepper.
Heat the oil in a pan and sweat the shallot, and garlic. Add to the vegetables in the salad bowl. Serve with the dressing.

Tip: You can replace the horseradish with wasabi paste if you prefer. In fact, this is a type of horseradish that is colored to look like the real wasabi root, which is much rarer.

PEAS WITH SPINACH AND FRESH MINT

SERVES 4

PREPARATION TIME 15 MINUTES

- 3 ⅓ cups (1 lb. 2 oz./500 g) shelled fresh peas
- 1 lb. 2 oz. (500 g) young spinach leaves
- ¼ cup (60 ml) extra virgin olive oil
- 1 shallot, finely chopped
- 1 garlic clove, finely chopped
- 8 fresh mint leaves, finely chopped
- ½ lemon
- Sea salt and freshly ground black pepper

Cook the peas for 2 minutes in boiling salted water until al dente. Drain. Heat the olive oil in a frying pan and sweat the shallot, garlic, and mint.
Add the young spinach leaves and cook until their water has evaporated.
Add the peas and cook for a further minute or two.
Season to taste with salt, pepper, and a drizzle of lemon juice.

Tip: Serve as a summer salad with mint pesto (see p. 77) and toasted whole-wheat bread.

BRUSCHETTA WITH CREAMED CARROT AND RAW TUNA

SERVES 12

PREPARATION TIME 20 MINUTES

- 3 $\frac{1}{2}$ oz. (100 g) fresh tuna (yellowfin), thinly sliced
- 10 tablespoons extra virgin olive oil
- 2 carrots, peeled and cut into small dice
- Scant $\frac{1}{2}$ cup (100 ml) vegetable stock (see p. 41)
- 1 teaspoon chopped fresh gingerroot
- 1 teaspoon coriander seeds
- Sea salt and freshly ground black pepper
- 1 teaspoon ground cardamom
- 6 dried sage leaves, finely crumbled
- 2 tablespoons lemon juice
- 1 multigrain baguette

Heat 2 tablespoons of the olive oil in a pan and sauté the diced carrot, without browning. Add the vegetable stock, chopped gingerroot, and coriander seeds. Simmer over a low heat until the liquid has evaporated. Puree using a hand-held blender or in a food processor.

Season the carrot puree with salt, pepper, cardamon, and half the dried sage.

Mix together 6 tablespoons of olive oil, the lemon juice, salt and pepper. Place the tuna slices in a dish and pour the marinade over it. Leave to marinate for 10 minutes.

Cut the baguette into thin slices. Heat the remaining 2 tablespoons of olive oil in a skillet and lightly fry the bread slices on both sides.

Spread the carrot puree onto each bread slice and top with a strip of tuna. Sprinkle with the remaining dried sage.

Tip: You can replace all or some of the tuna with salmon or smoked fish.
For vegetarians, the fish slices can be replaced with sweet and sour carrots.

ORECCHIETTE, ARUGULA, AND ROASTED TOMATO SALAD

SERVES 4

PREPARATION TIME: 40 MINUTES

- 16 small tomatoes, cut in half
- 5 tablespoons (75 ml) extra virgin olive oil
- 2 garlic cloves, finely chopped
- 1 shallot, finely chopped
- 1 teaspoon dried thyme
- 1 teaspoon ketchup
- 7 oz. (200 g) orecchiette (pasta)
- 7 oz. (200 g) arugula
- Juice and 1 teaspoon zest from 1 untreated lemon
- Sea salt and freshly ground black pepper

Preheat the oven to 250°F (120°C/gas 1/2).

Put the tomatoes in a bowl with 4 tablespoons of the olive oil, the garlic, shallot, thyme, and ketchup. Season them with salt and pepper.

Mix the seasoning into the tomatoes, then transfer them to a baking dish. Put the dish in the oven and cook for 40 minutes.

Cook the pasta in a large pan of boiling salted water until al dente (follow the package instructions for timing).

Drain the pasta, return it to the pan, and drizzle with a little olive oil to prevent it sticking. Let cool, then transfer it to a large salad bowl.

Wash and spin the arugula, then add it to the pasta, along with the remaining 1 tablespoon of olive oil, lemon juice and zest, and salt and pepper.

Finally, add the roasted tomatoes. Toss gently then serve.

Tip: Always cook your pasta in a large saucepan with a scant tablespoon of salt per liter of water. Stop the cooking process by adding a large glass of cold water to the cooking liquid, then drain the pasta.

YELLOW AND GREEN ZUCCHINI CURRY WITH CHIVES

SERVES 4

PREPARATION TIME 30 MINUTES

- 2 yellow zucchini
- 2 green zucchini
- 1 teaspoon coriander seeds
- 2 tablespoons ghee
- 1 tablespoon of chopped fresh gingerroot
- $1/2$ teaspoon ground cumin
- $1/2$ teaspoon ground turmeric
- $1/2$ teaspoon garam masala
- Scant 1 cup (200 ml) coconut milk
- Sea salt and freshly ground black pepper
- 15 fresh chives, snipped

Dry-fry the coriander seeds in a skillet then crush them using a pestle and mortar.

Cut each zucchini in quarters lengthwise. Remove any seeds and soft parts and cut the flesh in even-size pieces of about $3/4$ in. (2 cm).

Heat the ghee in a frying pan and sauté the gingerroot and cumin. Add the zucchini and sweat for 4–5 minutes.

Stir in the turmeric, coriander, and garam masala. Pour in the coconut milk, season with salt and pepper, cover, and cook for about 10 minutes until the vegetables are cooked through.

Add the chopped chives just before serving.

(Recipe photo on page 91.)

Note: The word *masala* in garam masala is a common one in the Indian subcontinent, meaning mixture, particularly of spices. In this sense a curry is a *masala*. The mix varies but usually includes turmeric, cloves, cumin, coriander, mustard seeds, and fenugreek.

ABOVE, TOP: In the window of the orangery, a few pots of white *Scilla peruviana*, part of the hyacinth family, are blooming.
ABOVE, BOTTOM: A basket of napkins is ready to be taken to the table in the garden. Of course, with busy schedules not everything can be organized in advance, and some details like place settings can be left to the last minute. If possible, it's important to plan to have all the essentials close at hand to avoid forgetting anything.

> **IT'S ALL GOOD, IT'S ALL BEAUTIFUL!
> I WOULD CALL IT HEALTHY COOKING,
> SEASONAL COOKING, LIGHT COOKING—THE
> SORT OF COOKING THAT I LOVE! THE
> VEGETABLES, SALADS, AND FRUITS ARE
> ALL FRESH FROM THE CHÂTEAU'S GARDENS.**
>
> *Marielle Labèque*

FACING PAGE: In between meals, beneath the shade of the apple tree, a view of the garden in the late afternoon sun reveals various shades of green while offering a quiet, meditative moment.
BELOW: Some often-overlooked ingredients in the kitchen can become some of the most important cooking staples. Bulgur is an example and one of the essential ingredients in our kitchen. Originally from the Middle East, bulgur is made from precooked wheat berries and takes about 20 minutes to prepare, so it's ideal for even the busiest schedules. Its high fiber content and low glucose levels make it a great substitute for rice or potatoes.

BULGUR WITH ROSEMARY AND SAGE

SERVES 4
PREPARATION TIME 25 MINUTES

- 1 teaspoon mustard seeds
- 1 teaspoon ground turmeric
- 1/2 teaspoon fenugreek
- 8–9 tablespoons extra virgin olive oil
- 1 shallot, finely chopped
- 1 garlic clove, finely chopped
- 1 tablespoon of chopped fresh gingerroot
- 16 sage leaves
- Leaves of 1 rosemary sprig, chopped
- 1 cup (7 oz./200 g) bulgur
- 2 cups (1 pint/500 ml) vegetable stock
- Sea salt and freshly ground black pepper
- Juice of 1/2 lemon

In a skillet, dry-fry the mustard seeds, turmeric, and fenugreek.
Add 2–3 tablespoons of oil and sweat the shallot, garlic, and gingerroot. Finely chop 8 sage leaves and add to the skillet, along with all the chopped rosemary. Pour in the bulgur and the stock. Simmer, covered, for 7 minutes.
Stir to separate the grains of bulgur and season with salt, pepper, 4 tablespoons of oil, and the lemon juice.
In a small skillet, fry the remaining sage leaves in 2 tablespoons of oil until crispy. Divide the bulgur into four bowls and garnish with the sage.

Tip: You can replace the bulgur with quinoa or einkorn wheat.

Leek and Broccoli Soup with Cardamom

SERVES 4

PREPARATION TIME 20 MINUTES

- 1 leek
- 1 celery stalk
- 10 ¹/₂ oz. (300 g) broccoli
- 1 small piece of butter
- 2 onions, finely chopped
- 1 garlic clove, finely chopped
- 4 cardamom pods
- 4 ¹/₄ cups (2 pints/1 liter) vegetable stock
- Sea salt and freshly ground black pepper

Trim the leek and finely chop both green and white parts, keeping them separate. Finely chop the celery. Separate the florets from the stem of the broccoli. Peel the stem, keeping only the central part, and chop finely. Carefully wash all the vegetables.

Heat the butter in a pan and sweat the white parts of the leeks with the onion, garlic, and celery. Then add the chopped broccoli stem and cardamom pods.

Pour in the vegetable stock, bring to a boil, then reduce the heat and simmer for 10 minutes.

Add the broccoli florets and the green parts of the leeks and cook for a further 5 minutes.

Puree the soup using a hand-held blender or in a food processor, then, if you wish, strain it. Season to taste with salt and pepper.

Tip: This recipe can also be used as a sauce to accompany fish. For a sauce, use only a third of the quantity of stock, i.e., 1 ¹/₂ cups (350 ml).

Facing page: Nature's creations inspire the style of many tables. A young meadow garden at the end of the summer displays sturdy grasses and bright wildflowers.
Pages 90 and 91: Lemons offer their rustic elegance to a table decoration alongside flowers in full bloom. Yellow and green zucchini curry is served (see recipe on page 85).

ROASTED MONKFISH FILLET WITH LEMON AND SPICES

SERVES 4

PREPARATION TIME: 35 MINUTES

- 2 lb. 3 oz. (1 kg) monkfish fillet
- 1 tablespoon coriander seeds
- 1 tablespoon cumin seeds
- 3 cardamom pods, crushed
- 1 large pinch ground star anise
- 1 teaspoon dried thyme
- 1 tablespoon zest and the juice of 1 lemon
- $1/2$ cup (120 ml) extra virgin olive oil, divided
- Sea salt and freshly ground black pepper

Preheat the oven 325°F (160°C/gas 3). In a skillet, dry-fry the coriander, cumin, and cardamom seeds, ground star anise, and dried thyme until they release their aromas. Tip the mixture into a blender and blend, adding the lemon zest and half the juice, 4 tablespoons of olive oil and some pepper. Transfer the mixture to a large plate.

Sprinkle the fish with salt, then roll it in this mixture. Heat a little oil in a skillet and brown the fish, then transfer it to a roasting pan. Roast in the oven for 15 minutes.

Remove from the oven, cover in aluminum foil and leave to rest at room temperature for 10 minutes.

Drizzle the cooked fish with a little olive oil and the remaining lemon juice.

Serve in slices or whole, accompanied by some broiled vegetables (e.g., zucchini, eggplant, or carrots).

Tip: You could also cook the fish on a grill.

Yellow Lentils and Baby Carrots with Ayurvedic Spices

SERVES 8
PREPARATION TIME 30 MINUTES

- 2 bunches (about 2 lb. / 1 kg) baby carrots
- 2 cups (1 pint/500 ml) vegetable stock
- $\frac{1}{2}$ teaspoon chopped fresh gingerroot
- 1 tablespoon mustard seeds
- $\frac{1}{2}$ teaspoon coriander seeds
- $\frac{1}{2}$ teaspoon cumin seeds
- $\frac{1}{2}$ teaspoon ground cinnamon
- $\frac{1}{2}$ teaspoon ground turmeric
- 2 cardamom pods, crushed
- Scant $\frac{1}{4}$ cup (50 ml) coconut oil
- 2 shallots, finely chopped
- 2 garlic cloves, finely chopped
- 1 $\frac{1}{4}$ cups (9 oz./250 g) yellow lentils, washed and drained
- Scant $\frac{1}{2}$ cup (100 ml) coconut milk
- 3 $\frac{1}{2}$ oz. (100 g) passata (sieved tomato pulp)
- 1 teaspoon Madras curry powder
- 1 kaffir lime leaf
- Sea salt and freshly ground black pepper
- Dash of lemon juice
- Leaves from 15 cilantro sprigs, chopped

Using a vegetable peeler, peel the carrots and thinly slice half of them. Cook the remainder in the stock, with the chopped gingerroot, until al dente. Remove with a slotted spoon, reserving the cooking liquid, and keep warm.

In a skillet, dry-fry the mustard, coriander, and cumin seeds, the ground cinnamon and turmeric, and the crushed cardamom pods. Put all the spices in a blender and grind to a powder.

Heat the coconut oil in a pan and sweat the shallot and garlic. Add the carrots and cook for a further 3 minutes. Add the lentils, $\frac{1}{3}$ of the cooking liquid, the coconut milk, passata, curry powder, and kaffir lime leaf. Cover the pan and simmer for 6 or 7 minutes. Check

regularly. Season with salt, pepper, and a dash of lemon juice.

To serve, transfer to a heated serving dish and sprinkle with the chopped cilantro.

Tip: Cooking times for lentils can vary: check the package instructions. If you prefer, you can replace them with mung beans or chickpeas.

ABOVE, BOTTOM: In the foreground, as fennel bulbs grow in the soil, their leafy greens produce a splendid sight above ground. In the background, asparagus leaves are still blooming after the asparagus season.
FACING PAGE: In addition to monkfish, other fish options are also delicious with this recipe, such as turbot, salmon, and sea bass. It's important to select a firm, flavorful fish and combine it with grilled vegetables such as zucchini, eggplant, and tomatoes.

SPICED CELERIAC CHUTNEY

SERVES 4

PREPARATION TIME 30 MINUTES

- 10 $^1/_2$ oz. (300 g) celeriac, peeled and diced into $^1/_4$ in. (6 mm) pieces
- 6 white celery stalks, diced into $^1/_4$ in. (6 mm) pieces
- 3 tablespoons extra virgin olive oil
- 1 white onion, finely chopped
- 1 garlic clove, finely chopped
- 1 tablespoon coriander seeds
- 1 tablespoon chopped fresh gingerroot
- 1 teaspoon grated fresh turmeric
- 1 teaspoon Madras curry powder
- Scant $^1/_2$ cup (100 ml) chicken or vegetable stock
- Scant $^1/_4$ cup (50 ml) cider vinegar
- Juice of 1 lemon plus 2 tablespoons zest
- 1 tablespoon palm sugar
- Sea salt and freshly ground black pepper

Heat the oil in a skillet and sweat the onion and garlic.

Crush the coriander seeds using a pestle and mortar, then dry-fry them in a skillet. Add the gingerroot, turmeric, and curry powder and cook until they begin to release their aromas.

Stir all these spices into the onion and garlic, along with the celeriac and celery. Sweat for a few minutes then pour over the stock, cover the pan, and simmer for 10 minutes.

Remove the lid and cook for a further five minutes or so until all the liquid has evaporated.

Add the cider vinegar, lemon zest and juice, and palm sugar and season with salt and pepper.

Tip: Serve hot or cold as a side dish. This can also be served on small rounds of toasted bread as an appetizer.

WATERZOOI CHICKEN CURRY (CHILDREN'S MENU)

SERVES 4

PREPARATION TIME 1 HOUR

- 4 free-range chicken legs
- 4 $^1/_4$ cups (2 pints/1 liter) vegetable stock
- 1 tablespoon ghee
- 1 white onion, chopped
- 1 garlic clove, finely chopped
- 1 white celery stick, chopped
- 1 Golden Delicious apple, peeled, cored, and diced
- 1 small fresh lemongrass stalk, chopped
- 1 tablespoon Madras curry powder
- 1 tablespoon ground turmeric
- Scant 1 cup (200 ml) coconut milk
- 1 bay leaf
- 1 kaffir lime leaf
- 1 green zucchini, cut into $^1/_2$ in. (1.5 cm) dice
- 1 yellow zucchini, cut into $^1/_2$ in. (1.5 cm) dice
- Sea salt and freshly ground black pepper
- Dash of lemon juice

Cut the chicken legs into two parts through the joint. Put them in a large pan, pour over the stock, and poach at a simmer for 20 minutes. Remove them from the pan, reserving the stock, and remove the skin.

Heat the ghee in a pan and sweat the onion, garlic, celery, apple, and lemongrass for a few minutes.

Sprinkle over the curry powder and turmeric. Pour in the coconut milk and a scant $^1/_2$ cup (100 ml) of the reserved cooking liquid. Add the bay leaf and kaffir lime leaf and simmer over a low heat, uncovered, for 20 minutes. Strain and return the liquid to the pan. Carefully add the zucchini and chicken to the strained sauce and simmer for 10 minutes. Season with salt, pepper, and a dash of lemon juice.

Tip: Use the remainder of the reserved stock to cook brown rice to accompany this dish, or use it in a risotto.

POINTED CABBAGE AND ROASTED TOMATO SALAD

SERVES 4

PREPARATION TIME 1 HOUR 10 MINUTES

- 1 small pointed cabbage, shredded
- 12 small roasted tomatoes (see p. 53)
- $^2/_3$ cup (3 $^1/_2$ oz./100 g) shelled fresh peas
- 2 tablespoons ghee or clarified butter
- $^1/_2$-in (1-cm) piece fresh gingerroot, grated
- 1 teaspoon black mustard seeds
- 1 teaspoon cumin seeds
- 1 kaffir lime leaf
- 1 garlic clove, finely chopped
- 2 tablespoons shredded coconut
- 1 teaspoon ground turmeric
- $^1/_2$ teaspoon garam masala
- Sea salt and freshly ground black pepper
- $^1/_2$ lemon (or lime)

Cook the peas for 2 minutes in boiling
salted water, then plunge them into iced
water.

Heat the ghee or clarified butter in a pan
and quickly stir-fry the gingerroot,
mustard seeds, cumin, and kaffir lime leaf.
Add the shredded cabbage and the garlic.
Cook for a few minutes, stirring to
prevent browning.

When the cabbage is translucent, add
the peas, shredded coconut, turmeric,
and garam masala.

Season with salt and pepper. Stir in
a dash of lemon juice and the roasted
tomatoes.

Tip: You can replace the pointed cabbage
with $^1/_2$ white cabbage.

In a corner of the garden, an abundance of pointed cabbage is growing. A popular
choice for soups and salads, cabbage is high in vitamins A and C and has several
important health benefits. Pointed cabbage is even said to help relieve headaches.

EGGPLANT SALAD WITH YOGURT AND CUCUMBER DRESSING

SERVES 4

PREPARATION TIME 30 MINUTES

- 2 eggplants
- 6–8 tablespoons extra virgin olive oil or ghee
- 1 shallot, finely chopped
- 1 garlic clove, finely chopped
- Freshly ground black pepper
- Scant ¹/₂ cup (100 ml) soy sauce
- 1 lemon
- 10 ¹/₂ oz. (300 g) mixed green salad leaves

For the yogurt and cucumber dressing:
- 1 small cucumber
- ¹/₂ teaspoon sesame seeds
- 1 tablespoon sesame oil
- ¹/₂ teaspoon white mustard seeds
- Scant 1 cup (200 ml) low-fat yogurt
- 1 tablespoon chopped fresh mint
- Zest of ¹/₂ lemon
- Sea salt

Peel the eggplants and cut them into 1 in. (2.5 cm) pieces.
Heat the olive oil or ghee in a pan and sweat the shallot and garlic.
Add the eggplant, pepper, and soy sauce and sauté. Continue to cook over a low heat, stirring regularly, for about 20 minutes. Stir in 3 or 4 tablespoons of lemon juice and keep warm.
To make the dressing, peel the cucumber, cut into quarters lengthwise, remove the seeds, and chop finely.
In a small skillet, dry-fry the sesame seeds until golden and put in a small bowl.
Add the sesame oil to the pan, heat, and gently fry the mustard seeds until lightly browned. Add to the bowl. Add the chopped cucumber to the bowl, along with the yogurt, mint, lemon zest, and salt.
In a salad bowl, mix together the mixed green salad leaves and the diced eggplant. Pour over the yogurt and cucumber dressing.

Tip: It is worth noting that you cannot overheat sesame oil. Its smoke point is in fact 350°F (177°C).

BAKED BREAM WITH FRESH HERB PESTO

SERVES 4

PREPARATION TIME 30 MINUTES

- Four 9 oz. (250 g) bream fillets
- 1 celery stalk, finely chopped
- Leaves of 4 thyme sprigs, finely chopped
- 8 sage leaves, finely chopped
- Sea salt and freshly ground black pepper
- 3 tablespoons extra virgin olive oil

For the pesto:
- 15 basil leaves
- 6 fresh mint leaves
- 1 tablespoon chopped fresh tarragon
- 1 tablespoon chopped fresh cilantro
- 1 tablespoon pine nuts
- 2 tablespoons grated Parmesan
- 2 garlic cloves, finely chopped
- Scant ¹/₄ cup (50 ml) extra virgin olive oil
- Scant ¹/₄ cup (50 ml) argan oil
- 1 lemon
- Sea salt and freshly ground black pepper

Preheat the oven to 300°F (150°C/gas 2). Put the fish in a roasting pan and season with the celery, thyme, sage, salt, and pepper. Add a little olive oil, put in the oven, and bake for 15 minutes.
Meanwhile, make the pesto, put the herbs, pine nuts, grated Parmesan, garlic, olive and argan oils, and the juice of ¹/₂ the lemon in a food processor or blender, and mix until you have a green puree.
Season with salt and pepper.
Remove the fish from the oven, squeeze over the remaining ¹/₂ lemon, and serve with the pesto.

ABOVE, TOP: One of the key ingredients in the recipe for dorade is argan oil, which is made from pressing the seeds of a nut produced by argan trees in Morocco. This type of oil is well known for its fine taste and nutritional qualities. It's best to keep argan oil in cool conditions in a dark bottle that's not exposed to direct sunlight.
ABOVE, BOTTOM: Bright lavender chive blossoms blooming in the garden have a cheerful, pleasing color.

ABOVE, FACING PAGE, AND PAGES 102–103: A selection of fruits and compotes is served for breakfast on an outdoor terrace at s'Gravenwezel. When creating a breakfast table, I often serve a variety of fruit, yogurt, and bread. Compote is ideal as it can be mixed with grains such as oats or quinoa or used as jam with bread and toast. For more savory options, I also serve grilled, warm tomatoes, Araucana eggs, and cheeses in the morning.

POACHED APPLES WITH TURMERIC AND BLUEBERRIES

SERVES 4

PREPARATION TIME 25 MINUTES

- 2 apples (Golden Delicious or Pink Lady)
- Scant 1 cup (200 ml) water
- 1 teaspoon grated fresh turmeric
- $^1/_2$ lemongrass stalk
- $^1/_4$ cinnamon stick
- Scant $^1/_2$ cup (100 ml) agave syrup
- 2 tablespoons dried blueberries (or cranberries)
- 1 lemon

Peel the apples, cut in quarters, and remove the cores. Cut each quarter into three. To make the syrup, put the water in a pan with the turmeric and lemongrass and bring to a boil. Add the cinnamon and the agave syrup, reduce the heat, and simmer for 10 minutes.

Filter the syrup then return it to the pan. Add the apples and blueberries and poach for 5–10 minutes at 194°F (90°C). Remove the fruit from the poaching liquid and sprinkle with lemon juice.

Tip: Try serving these apples with muesli and yogurt, sprinkled with toasted flaxseeds and pumpkin seeds.

APRICOT AND PASSION FRUIT COMPOTE

MAKES 2 PINTS (1 LITER)

PREPARATION TIME 40 MINUTES

- 1 lb. 2 oz. (500 g) organic dried apricots
- Scant $^1/_2$ cup (100 ml) water
- 1–2 tablespoons lemon zest
- 1 cup ($^1/_2$ pint/250 ml) passion fruit juice
- 1 cup ($^1/_2$ pint/250 ml) apple juice

Cut the apricots into $^1/_4$ in. (6 mm) strips. Put them in a pan with the water and lemon zest and simmer, covered, for 15 minutes.

Add the fruit juices, and simmer, still covered, for a further 20 minutes. Puree using a hand-held blender or in a food processor until smooth.

If you wish, you can add some passion fruit seeds.

Tip: To make the passion fruit juice yourself, you will need about 15 fresh passion fruits.

RHUBARB COMPOTE WITH STAR ANISE AND RED BERRY JUICE

SERVES 4

PREPARATION TIME 20 MINUTES (PLUS OVERNIGHT RESTING TIME)

- 1 tablespoon orange zest
- 4 rhubarb stalks
- Scant 1 cup (200 ml) red berry juice
- $^2/_3$ cup (150 ml) agave syrup or rice syrup
- 2 star anise
- $^1/_2$ teaspoon ground cinnamon
- $^1/_2$ teaspoon ground aniseed

Blanch the orange zest for 20 seconds in a little boiling water and repeat this process five times, changing the blanching water and rinsing the zest under running water after each blanching.

To make the syrup, put the fruit juice, agave syrup, blanched orange zest, star anise, cinnamon, and ground aniseed in a pan and heat, but without boiling, for 10 minutes.

Carefully peel the rhubarb, removing all the stringy pieces, and cut into pieces 1 $^1/_4$–1 $^1/_2$ in. (3–4 cm) long. Add to the syrup and poach at about 140°F (60°C) for 15 minutes.

Let cool, then cover with plastic wrap and refrigerate overnight for the flavors to infuse.

Tip: This dish can be served for breakfast or to accompany a chocolate dessert.

PINEAPPLE WITH SAFFRON AND LEMON

SERVES 4

PREPARATION TIME 1 HOUR

- 1 small fresh pineapple
- 1 teaspoon coriander seeds
- Scant ¹/₂ cup (100 ml) water
- Scant ¹/₂ cup (100 ml) agave syrup
- 1–2 tablespoons lemon zest
- 1 teaspoon ground turmeric
- Pinch of saffron threads

Peel the pineapple, cut it into quarters vertically, and remove the hard core. Slice it into 1 in. (2.5 cm) thick slices. In a skillet, dry-fry the coriander seeds, then crush them using a pestle and mortar.

Put the water in a pan with the agave syrup, lemon zest, turmeric, and saffron, and bring to a boil. Turn off the heat and add the coriander.

Add the pineapple to the syrup and poach it for 45 minutes over a low heat, until all the liquid has evaporated.

PEARS POACHED IN SAFFRON

SERVES 4

PREPARATION TIME 25 MINUTES

- Zest of 1 orange
- 4 pears (Bartlett or Comice)
- Scant 1 cup (200 ml) water
- Scant ¹/₂ cup (100 ml) rice syrup
- 4 teaspoons ginger syrup
- 1 tablespoon chopped fresh gingerroot
- ¹/₂ teaspoon ground cardamom
- Pinch of saffron threads
- 1 lemon

Blanch the orange zest for 20 seconds in a little boiling water and repeat this process five times, changing the blanching water and rinsing the zest under running water after each blanching.

Put the water in a pan with the rice syrup, ginger syrup, chopped fresh gingerroot, cardamom, and blanched orange zest. Bring to the boil, then reduce the heat and simmer for 5 minutes. Strain this liquid.

Peel the pears and cut each vertically into eight equal parts. Trim and remove the cores. Add the pears to the syrup, along with the saffron threads, and poach for 10–15 minutes, depending on the ripeness of the pears. Remove the pears from the syrup and sprinkle with lemon juice.

Serve the pears, cold or hot, with a little of the cooking liquid.

Tip: The syrup can be kept in an airtight container in the fridge for up to two weeks. You can use the same recipe for apples, peaches, or apricots.

MANGOES WITH YOGURT

SERVES 4

PREPARATION TIME 35 MINUTES

- 4 large orange-fleshed mangoes
- 4 teaspoons ginger syrup
- 1 ¹/₃ cups (400 ml) low-fat yogurt
- 1 lemon or lime
- 1 teaspoon grated fresh gingerroot
- ¹/₂ teaspoon grated fresh turmeric
- Pinch of ground cinnamon
- Pinch of ground cardamom

Stir the ginger syrup into the yogurt. Peel and pit the mangoes and dice them into ³/₄ in. (2 cm) pieces. Put in a dish. In a bowl, mix the lemon or lime juice with the various spices, pour over the mango, and let marinate for 30 minutes. Stir in the yogurt and serve.

Tip: This dish can be sprinkled with various oilseeds, such as sunflower seeds, flaxseeds, pumpkin seeds, and pine nuts.

FACING PAGE: A selection of herb-infused iced teas is served on a warm afternoon in Venice. To create different flavors, Patrick and I use a concentration of herbs along with lemon and ginger and then add a separate fruit juice such as grapefruit, blood orange, or apple to offer a distinctive, refreshing choice of tastes.

LEMON TARTLETS

MAKES 24 TARTLETS (OF 1 ¼ IN./3 CM
DIAMETER)
PREPARATION TIME 1 HOUR, PLUS 1 HOUR
RESTING TIME FOR THE PASTRY

For the rich tart pastry:
- 2 cups (7 oz./200 g) all-purpose flour
- Pinch of salt
- ¼ cup (1 ¾ oz./50 g) superfine granulated sugar
- 2 teaspoons (5 g) vanilla sugar
- ⅔ cup (1 ¾ oz./50 g) ground almonds
- 1 ¼ sticks (5 oz./140 g) butter, slightly softened
- 1 egg, beaten

For the lemon cream:
- 2 tablespoons lemon zest
- 5 ½ tablespoons (2 ¾ oz./80 g) butter, softened
- ½ cup (3 ½ oz./100 g) superfine granulated sugar
- Juice of 2 lemons
- 1 egg plus 2 egg yolks, beaten

To make the rich tart pastry, in a bowl, stir together the flour, salt, sugar, vanilla sugar, and ground almonds. Incorporate the butter by hand. Add the egg and mix until you have a crumbly dough. Cover and refrigerate for 1 hour.
Preheat the oven to 325°F (160°C/gas 3). Roll out the pastry to about ⅛ in. (3 mm) thick and cut out small circles using a small cookie cutter.
Use these rounds to fill the holes of two muffin pans, then place in the oven for 5 minutes. Once the tartlet cases are cooked, remove to a cooling rack to cool.
To make the lemon cream, in a pan, work the lemon zest into the softened butter using a fork.
Add all the remaining ingredients and bring to a boil, beating continuously for a minute.
Transfer the mixture to a bowl, cover with plastic wrap to prevent a skin forming, and let cool.
Pour the lemon cream into the tartlet cases until nearly filled.

Tip: Serve these tartlets with Rhubarb Compote (see p. 100) and sprinkled with chopped fresh mint or cinnamon basil.

AYURVEDIC-STYLE QUINOA

SERVES 4
PREPARATION TIME 20 MINUTES

- ⅔ cup (2 ¾ oz./80 g) quinoa
- ⅔ cup (160 ml) salted water
- 1 teaspoon ground turmeric
- ½ teaspoon ground cinnamon
- ½ teaspoon ground cardamom
- 1 tablespoon dried blueberries
- 1 tablespoon currants
- ½ apple
- Juice of ½ lemon

Wash and drain the quinoa. Bring the salted water to a boil in a pan, add the quinoa and spices. Cover and cook over a low heat for 9–10 minutes. Stir in the dried blueberries and currants.
Just before serving, grate the apple over the top and sprinkle with the lemon juice.

Tip: You can replace the quinoa with oats, rye, or bulgur if you prefer.

AUTUMN

Many of us associate the transition between summer and autumn with the transformation of leaves and the poetry of their changing colors. It's one of my favorite times of year. As the trees and their branches drop a collection of leaves that dance toward the earth, the soil offers gifts in return. These arrive in the form of some of the richest flavors of the year, like the hearty tastes of squash, mushrooms, and a variety of root vegetables like parsnip that are the perfect accompaniment to many dishes. The menus of the season help bring the mind and body closer to the earth and begin to warm and soothe the body as the temperature starts to cool. Just as much as on the plate, I like to use the products of the season to enhance the feeling of a table or room, and even a hallway. The soft curves and natural textures of pumpkin and other squashes add a touch of refinement to please the eye.

FACING PAGE: The garden's transition from bright greens in summer to deep reds and rich browns in autumn offers a series of beautiful moments. During walks, I gather branches and leaves to complement flower decorations or add the spirit of the season to the table.

RIGHT: A chopped pointed cabbage is perfect for soups and salads or sautéed as a side dish.

PAGES 110–111: Dinner in the cellar is taken next to the open fire with a harvest of squash and pumpkins placed on the round table.

> 66 SHE KNOWS HOW TO BLEND
> NATURAL PRODUCTS SO THAT
> THE TASTE IS NEVER SMOTHERED BUT
> IS ENHANCED; THE SAME BALANCE
> GRACES HER TABLE ARRANGEMENTS.

Martine Dornier

A selection of commonly used spices and ingredients in our kitchen, including fresh turmeric, galangal root, and cinnamon, is placed on a Korean tray. In the small bowl is a mix of ayurvedic spices that we use frequently to add a boost of flavor and balance to many dishes. Some wonderful ayurvedic spice mixtures are available in stores and, after experimenting with Patrick, we've developed one that we love. This mixture is created using a five-spice blend, including fresh lemon grass, ginger, galangal root, and turmeric, along with crushed coriander seeds. Used in several recipes throughout the book, this blend can be refrigerated and is the ideal choice to enrich the taste of a wide variety of vegetables, and can also be tossed with rice, or used to season fish before placing in the oven.

BUTTERCUP SQUASH, BLACK SALSIFY, AND CARROT STEW

SERVES 4
PREPARATION TIME 40 MINUTES

- 2 lb. 3 oz. (1 kg) black salsify
- Scant ¹/₂ cup (100 ml) vinegar
- 1 small buttercup squash
- 2 carrots, peeled
- 1 ¹/₄ cups (300 ml) vegetable stock
- 1 small piece of butter
- 2 shallots, finely chopped
- 1 garlic clove, finely chopped
- 3 bay leaves
- 8 juniper berries
- 1 thyme sprig
- 8 sage leaves
- Sea salt, freshly ground black pepper, and freshly grated nutmeg

Wash and peel the black salsify using a vegetable peeler. Put them in a bowl, cover them with water, and add the vinegar. Set aside.
Peel the squash, cut in half, and remove the seeds. Set aside 1 lb. 2 oz. (500 g) of the flesh for the puree and cut the remainder, as well as the carrots and black salsify, into diamond shapes about 1 in. (2.5 cm) long.
Dice the remaining 1 lb. 2 oz. (500 g) of squash, and cook it in two-thirds of the vegetable stock. Puree it using a hand-held blender or in a food processor. Set aside.
Heat the butter in a pan and sweat the shallots and garlic. Add the cut carrots, salsify, and squash. Add the bay leaves, juniper berries, thyme, and sage. Pour over the remaining vegetable stock, cover, and simmer over a low heat until the vegetables are cooked (test with a fork). Stir in the squash puree, grate in some nutmeg, and adjust the seasoning if necessary.

LAMB'S LETTUCE, BUTTERNUT SQUASH, BEET, WILD MUSHROOM, AND MIXED NUT SALAD

SERVES 4

PREPARATION TIME 30 MINUTES

- 1 large beet (raw)
- 3 ¹/₂ oz. (100 g) flesh from a butternut squash
- 7 oz. (200 g) wild mushrooms
- 7 oz. (200 g) lamb's lettuce
- 2 tablespoons extra virgin olive oil
- 2 tablespoons mixed nuts (e.g., walnuts, cashews, almonds, pecans)
- 1 small piece of butter
- 1 garlic clove, finely chopped
- 1 shallot, finely chopped
- 1 tablespoon chopped parsley
- Sea salt and freshly ground black pepper

For the dressing:

- ¹/₄ cup (60 ml) extra virgin olive oil
- 2 tablespoons hazelnut oil
- 3 tablespoons sherry or cider vinegar
- 1 teaspoon wholegrain mustard
- 1 teaspoon honey
- 1 teaspoon ground star anise
- Sea salt and freshly ground black pepper

Peel the beet, rinse it several times, and julienne it.

Julienne the butternut squash. Carefully brush clean the wild mushrooms, rinse rapidly under running water, then dry them. Trim, wash, and spin or pat dry the lamb's lettuce.

In a large salad bowl, mix together the lamb's lettuce, beet, and butternut squash.

Heat some oil in a skillet and gently fry the nuts until golden. Remove the nuts from the skillet and coarsely chop them. Add the butter to the skillet, then sauté the mushrooms, garlic, and shallot over a high heat. Add the parsley and season with salt and pepper.

To make the dressing, put the olive and hazelnut oils, vinegar, mustard, honey, star anise, and salt and pepper in a bowl and whisk together.

Pour the dressing over the salad and toss. Add the mushrooms and mixed nuts to the bowl. Serve immediately.

Tip: Serve this salad as an accompaniment to chicken, turkey, or oily fish (e.g., salmon or tuna).

YELLOW TURNIPS WITH GINGER ROOT

SERVES 4

PREPARATION TIME 25 MINUTES

- 12 medium-size yellow turnips
- 1 teaspoon coriander seeds
- $^1/_2$ teaspoon mustard seeds
- Scant $^1/_4$ cup (50 ml) extra virgin olive oil
- 1 large shallot, finely chopped
- 1 garlic clove, finely chopped
- $^1/_2$ in. (1 cm) piece fresh gingerroot, finely chopped
- $^1/_2$ teaspoon ground turmeric
- Scant 1 cup (200 ml) vegetable stock
- 2 kaffir lime leaves
- 1 tablespoon honey
- Scant $^1/_2$ cup (100 ml) cider vinegar
- Sea salt and freshly ground black pepper

In a small skillet, dry-fry the coriander and mustard seeds until they begin to color, then remove them immediately. Using a vegetable peeler, peel the turnips, and cut each one into 8 wedges.
Heat the oil in a pan and sweat the shallot, garlic, and turnip.
Then add coriander, mustard, gingerroot, and turmeric. Stir, then pour in the stock and add the kaffir lime leaves. Cover the pan and simmer for 20 minutes.
Stir in the honey and vinegar and cook for a further 1–2 minutes. Remove from the heat but leave covered.
Season with salt and pepper before serving.

Tip: Serve hot as an accompaniment to broiled chicken or lamb, or warm with a green salad.

TURNIPS WITH FRESH HERB OIL

SERVES 4

PREPARATION TIME 20 MINUTES

- 8 white turnips
- 1 oz. (30 g) flat-leaf parsley
- 1 oz. (30 g) chervil
- 1 oz. (30 g) baby spinach leaves
- $^1/_3$ oz. (10 g) fresh tarragon
- $^1/_3$ oz. (10 g) watercress
- $^1/_3$ oz. (10 g) chives
- 1 $^1/_4$ cups (300 ml) vegetable stock
- $^1/_2$ cup (120 ml) extra virgin olive oil
- 1 garlic clove, finely chopped
- Juice of 1 lemon
- Sea salt and freshly ground black pepper

Remove the leaves from the different herbs and salad leaves, reserving the stalks. Wash the leaves and pat dry. Using a vegetable peeler, peel the turnips, leaving about 1 in. (2.5 cm) of the stalks intact. Cut them in half vertically.
Put the stock and the herb stalks in a pan and bring to a boil. Add the turnips and simmer for about 10 minutes until just cooked.
Blanch the herb leaves in boiling salted water for 30 seconds, then plunge them immediately into iced water.
Squeeze them to eliminate all the water. Mix the herbs with the olive oil, garlic, and lemon juice and season to taste with salt and pepper.
Serve the turnips hot or warm, sprinkled with the herb oil.

Tip: You can make a multicolored version of this dish using beets and yellow turnips.

ABOVE, BOTTOM: Wild mushroom hunting is an exciting activity that yields delicious results in autumn. Whether foraging at the local market or in a forest, mushrooms can be a perfect accompaniment to many dishes or served alone with olive oil and simple seasoning.
PAGES 116 AND 117: A collection of salads and side dishes are waiting to be served from the cellar, including white radish with herbs.

PUMPKIN RISOTTO

SERVES 4

PREPARATION TIME 30 MINUTES

- 1 pumpkin (approximately 2 lb. 3 oz./1 kg)
- 2 tablespoons extra virgin olive oil
- 1 tablespoon grated fresh gingerroot
- 1 teaspoon ground turmeric
- 1 teaspoon curry powder
- 2 shallots, finely chopped
- 2 garlic cloves, finely chopped
- Rounded $^1/_2$ cup (4 $^1/_4$ oz./120 g) arborio rice
- Scant 1 cup (200 ml) dry white wine
- Sea salt and freshly ground black pepper
- 1 $^1/_4$–1 $^2/_3$ cups (300–400 ml) vegetable stock
- 1 small piece of butter
- $^1/_4$ cup (1 $^3/_4$ oz./50 g) grated Parmesan
- 1 tablespoon chopped fresh tarragon

Peel the pumpkin and dice it into $^1/_2$ in. (1 cm) pieces.

Heat a tablespoon of oil in a pan and brown the pumpkin along with the gingerroot, turmeric, curry powder, and half the chopped shallot and garlic over a high heat. Set aside.

In another pan, heat the remaining 1 tablespoon of oil and sweat the remaining shallot and garlic until translucent. Add the rice and cook until it, too, becomes translucent. Stir in the white wine and simmer over a low heat until nearly all of it has evaporated. Add the vegetable stock a ladleful at a time.

After about 10 minutes, add the browned pumpkin. Continue cooking until the rice is cooked (this will take about a further 10 minutes).

Remove the pan from the heat and add the butter, Parmesan, and tarragon. Stir well and check the seasoning.

Serve as a side order or to accompany fish.

BUTTERNUT SQUASH MARINATED IN TARRAGON

SERVES 4

PREPARATION TIME 20 MINUTES

- 1 butternut squash
- Sea salt and freshly ground black pepper
- Leaves from 1 tarragon sprig
- 4–5 tablespoons extra virgin olive oil
- 3 tablespoons hazelnut oil
- Juice of 1 lemon
- $^1/_2$ teaspoon wholegrain mustard
- 1 small shallot, finely chopped
- 1 garlic clove, finely chopped
- 1 teaspoon sunflower seeds
- 1 teaspoon pumpkin seeds
- 1 teaspoon pine nuts
- 2 dried sage leaves

Using a paring knife, peel the butternut squash, cut it in half lengthwise, and remove the seeds. Cut the flesh into $^1/_8$ in. (3 mm) thick slices.

Blanch for 2 minutes in 2 pints (1 liter) of boiling salted water. Drain and pat dry with paper towel, then place in a serving dish and season with salt and pepper.

To make the dressing, set aside a few tarragon leaves to use as a garnish and chop the remainder. In a bowl, mix together the olive and hazelnut oils, lemon juice, mustard, shallot, garlic, and chopped tarragon leaves, and pour over the butternut squash.

In a small skillet, dry-fry the sunflower and pumpkin seeds and pine nuts. Chop them finely with the sage. Sprinkle this mixture over the butternut squash and garnish with the reserved tarragon leaves. Serve cold.

FACING PAGE: The garden produces an abundance of pumpkins and butternut squash that provide pleasant tastes and decoration throughout the season. Every year at our home, we choose a selection of seeds to grow various orange, red, and yellow pumpkins, as well as butternut varieties. Recently, we've been trying Japanese squash as well. One requirement in our garden is that we only plant and grow edible varieties.

> " MAY VERVOORDT'S ENTERTAINING COULD ALSO BE SUBTITLED *"L'ART QUI CACHE L'ART"*: THE EXQUISITELY DECORATED TABLE (WHEREVER IT MIGHT BE—AND IT IS ALMOST NEVER IN THE SAME PLACE), PRESENTS FOOD THAT IS UNIQUE, UTTERLY DELICIOUS, SURPRISING, BEAUTIFUL TO LOOK AT, AND FEATHER-LIGHT.

Robert Carsen

The appeal of pumpkins and squash stems from their naturally elegant shapes, textures, and colors. They are as pleasing to look at as they are on the plate. Whether they are in the garden or in the kitchen, or around the home adding style to an entryway, staircase, or windowsill, their refined simplicity adds an attractive visual dimension to any experience. In the image below, pumpkins are growing in the patch. When preparing pumpkins for many recipes, it's a useful technique to separate the seeds. Once washed and dried, it's possible to toast them and save for later use in soups, salads, or to eat as a snack as a delicious alternative to other common snacks such as chips.

CREAMED BUTTERNUT SQUASH WITH GINGERROOT AND TURMERIC

SERVES 4
PREPARATION TIME 20 MINUTES

- 1 butternut squash
- 1 carrot
- $^1/_2$ teaspoon coriander seeds
- $^1/_2$ teaspoon curry powder
- 1 cardamom pod, crushed
- $^1/_2$ cinnamon stick
- 1 small piece of butter
- 1 shallot, finely chopped
- 1 garlic clove, finely chopped
- 1 small red chili pepper, seeded and finely chopped
- 1 tablespoon of chopped fresh gingerroot
- 1 teaspoon fresh chopped turmeric
- Scant 1 cup (200 ml) chicken or vegetable stock
- Juice of $^1/_2$ lemon
- Sea salt and freshly ground black pepper

Using a paring knife, peel the butternut squash, remove the seeds, and chop the flesh coarsely.

Peel and coarsely chop the carrot.

In a skillet, dry-fry the coriander seeds, curry powder, crushed cardamom pod, and the $^1/_2$ cinnamon stick until golden. Transfer to a plate.

Melt the butter in a pan and sweat the shallot, garlic, chili pepper, and diced carrot and butternut squash. Stir in the gingerroot and turmeric.

Pour over the stock and cook, uncovered, stirring regularly, until all the stock has evaporated.

Remove and discard the cinnamon stick, then puree using a hand-held blender or in a food processor.

Add the lemon juice and season with salt and pepper.

Originally from the Middle East and Asia, and now grown in many other parts of the world, purple carrots are not as popular as the more famous orange and yellow varieties, and yet have more beta carotene. Together with beet, both are a rich source of antioxidants. I love experimenting with rarely used vegetables like these carrots, as well as black radish, rutabaga, and others.

RUTABAGA, WILD MUSHROOM, AND HUMMUS "TARTLETS"

SERVES 4

PREPARATION TIME 1 HOUR

For the homemade hummus
- 1 ¹/₂ cups (3 ¹/₂ oz./100 g) cooked or canned chickpeas, with cooking liquid or brine
- ¹/₂ garlic clove, finely chopped
- 1 tablespoons extra virgin olive oil
- Juice of ¹/₂ lemon
- Sea salt and freshly ground black pepper
- Scant ¹/₂ cup (100 ml) sour cream
- 1 tablespoon chopped fresh flat-leaf parsley

For the "tartlets"
- 1 rutabaga
- 1 ²/₃ cups (400 ml) vegetable stock
- ¹/₄ cup (1 ³/₄ oz./50 g) green lentils
- 9 oz. (250 g) wild mushrooms
- 1 small piece of butter
- 1 shallot, finely chopped
- 1 garlic clove, finely chopped
- Sea salt and freshly ground black pepper
- 2 tablespoons chopped fresh flat-leaf parsley

For the hummus, if using canned chick peas reheat them in their brine, or if using dried cook them according to the instructions on the package. Leave to cool a little. Puree the lukewarm chickpeas with the cooking liquid and the garlic in a blender or food processor, adding the oil and lemon juice a little at a time. Season with salt and pepper.

Let rest in a cool place for 30 minutes then stir in the sour cream and parsley using a spatula.

For the "tartlets," peel the rutabaga and cut it into ¹/₄-in. (6-mm) thick slices. Cook in the stock until just done. Remove the rutabaga slices using a slotted spoon and set aside.

Wash the lentils thoroughly, then add them to the stock and cook for about 20 minutes. Keep warm.

Trim the mushrooms and wipe them

clean with a damp cloth. Heat the butter in a frying pan and sauté the mushrooms with the shallot and garlic. Season with salt and pepper, sprinkle with the parsley and keep hot.

To serve, lay a slice of rutabaga in the center of a plate. Spread some lentils on top, then a quenelle of hummus. Finish with the mushrooms and the remainder of the lentils. Season with salt and pepper.

Tip: Form the quenelles between two soupspoons held "head to head." To prevent the ingredients sticking, dip the spoons in hot water first.

MEADOW MUSHROOM AND BLACK RADISH SALAD

SERVES 4

PREPARATION TIME 40 MINUTES

- 1 lb. (500 g) meadow mushrooms
- 1 long black radish (8–10 in./20–25 cm)
- 1 ¼ cups (300 ml) vegetable stock
- Scant ½ cup (100 ml) soy sauce
- 1 small piece of salted butter
- 1 garlic clove, finely chopped
- 1 large shallot, finely chopped
- 2 tablespoons chopped flat-leaf parsley
- Sea salt and freshly ground black pepper
- 1 lemon
- 1 bunch of watercress
- 10 ½ oz. (300 g) mixed young salad leaves
- 3 tablespoons extra virgin olive oil
- 3 tablespoons virgin sesame oil

Using a vegetable peeler, peel the black radish and cut it into ⅛-in. (3-mm) thick slices. Poach these slices in the vegetable stock and soy sauce until al dente. Quickly rinse the mushrooms and pat them dry, then cut them into slices. Heat the butter in a frying-pan and sauté the mushrooms, garlic, and shallot. When cooked, add the parsley and season to taste.
Remove the pan from the heat and add the juice of ½ lemon.

Wash and trim the watercress and other salad leaves, place in a large salad bowl, and season with salt, pepper, olive oil, and a drizzle of lemon juice.
Transfer the black radish slices from their cooking liquid to the salad bowl and drizzle with the sesame oil.
Add the mushrooms to the bowl and toss to combine.

Tip: Depending on the season, you could replace the meadow mushrooms with ceps or cheaper button mushrooms.

SHALLOTS ROASTED WITH LEMON, THYME, AND SAGE

SERVES 4

PREPARATION TIME 1 HOUR

- 16 large shallots
- 2 garlic cloves
- 2 untreated lemons, cut into small pieces
- 2 sage sprigs
- 3 fresh thyme sprigs (lemon if possible)
- ½ cup (120 ml) extra virgin olive oil
- Sea salt and freshly ground black pepper

Preheat the oven to 250°F (120°C/gas 1/2). Crush the unpeeled garlic cloves with the side of a knife blade.
Put the unpeeled shallots into a roasting pan with all the other ingredients and mix together.
Place the pan in the oven and roast for 1 hour, shaking the pan at regular intervals.

Tip: Serve these roasted shallots as an accompaniment to roast meat, or puree and serve with game.

PAGES 124 AND 125: A rutabaga, wild mushroom, and hummus "tartlet" is prepped for a large gathering in Venice at Palazzo Alvera to celebrate the opening of an exhibition (see recipe on page 122). Typical Venetian biscuits are a creative and edible table decoration and can be prepared in various sizes and shapes to match any theme.

ROAST PARSNIPS AND POINTED CABBAGE WITH HAZELNUTS

SERVES 4

PREPARATION TIME 30 MINUTES

- 4 small parsnips
- 1 small pointed cabbage
- $^1/_2$ cup (120 ml) extra virgin olive oil
- 2 shallots, finely chopped
- 2 garlic cloves, finely chopped
- 1 thyme sprig
- 4 sage leaves
- Sea salt and freshly ground black pepper
- 1 tablespoon hazelnuts (whole)
- $^1/_2$ teaspoon cumin seeds
- $^1/_2$ teaspoon ground turmeric
- $^1/_2$ teaspoon ground cinnamon
- $^1/_2$ teaspoon Madras curry powder
- Scant $^1/_2$ cup (100 ml) coconut milk
- $^1/_2$ teaspoon red curry paste
- Juice of 1 lemon

Preheat the oven to 350°F (180°C/gas 4). Using a vegetable peeler, peel the parsnips and cut them in half lengthwise. In a roasting pan, combine the parsnips with half the olive oil, the chopped shallot and garlic, the thyme and sage, salt and pepper. Roast them in the oven for 20 minutes. Shake the pan occasionally during the roasting time.

Meanwhile, shred the cabbage, wash, and spin or pat dry.

In a pan, dry-fry the hazelnuts, cumin, turmeric, cinnamon, and Madras curry powder. Add the remaining olive oil and the shredded cabbage, then pour in the coconut milk and stir in the curry paste. Cook for a few minutes, stirring, then add the lemon juice. Cover and cook for 5 minutes.

Divide the cabbage mixture and the roast parsnips between four heated soup plates.

Tip: Try substituting parsley root, potatoes, pumpkin, or a mixture of these vegetables for the parsnips.

CURRIED CHINESE ARTICHOKES

SERVES 4

PREPARATION TIME 15 MINUTES

- 14 oz. (400 g) Chinese artichokes
- Coarse salt
- 1 tablespoon all-purpose flour
- Scant $^1/_2$ cup (100 ml) white wine vinegar
- Scant cup (200 ml) soy cream
- 1 teaspoon curry powder
- 1 lemon
- Sea salt and freshly ground black pepper

Clean the Chinese artichokes by scrubbing them with coarse salt in paper towel. Rinse thoroughly. Prepare a *blanc*: fill a pan with enough water to cover the artichokes, then whisk in the flour, vinegar, and salt and pepper. Bring to a boil, then add the Chinese artichokes and simmer for about 10 minutes until al dente. Put the soy cream in a heavy-bottomed pan and heat until it has reduced by half. Stir in the curry powder. Season the soy cream with the lemon juice, salt, and pepper, then add the cooked Chinese artichokes.

Tip: Serve on their own or with a poached egg, or to accompany fish or meat.

FACING PAGE AND ABOVE: I'm often drawn to forgotten or unusual vegetables, such as the types featured on these pages, parsnip and Chinese artichoke. Also known as crosne, I love the beautiful shape of Chinese artichokes. With a crunchy texture and earthy taste that's similar to that of Jerusalem artichokes, Chinese artichokes are often available from November through March and may be eaten in salads or with other cooked vegetables. I love to serve them in various sauces as well, such as curry.

ABOVE, BOTTOM: A wooden bowl is filled with Jerusalem artichokes. A delicious tuber that we use often, the flowering plant is similar to a sunflower and produces beautiful yellow blossoms in late summer and early autumn that are perfect for kitchen arrangements.
PAGES 130 AND 131: A collection of dried spices and celeriac is presented after slow cooking. Both are ingredients that I use to make Baked Celeriac with Nuts and Grains (see recipe on page 155).

BRAISED RED ENDIVES

SERVES 4

PREPARATION TIME 40 MINUTES

- 8 red endives
- 1 small piece of butter
- Sea salt, freshly ground black pepper, and freshly grated nutmeg
- Scant $1/2$ cup (100 ml) of water
- $1/2$ tablespoon sugar cane or scant $1/4$ cup (50 ml) agave syrup
- Juice of $1/2$ lemon
- 2 tablespoons extra virgin olive oil
- 3 juniper berries, finely chopped

Using a sharp paring knife, remove the central, cone-shaped, bitter part of the endives, then cut the endives in quarters lengthwise.
Heat the butter in a frying pan and cook the endives for a few minutes until golden. Season to taste with salt, pepper, and nutmeg.
Add a scant $1/2$ cup (100 ml) of water, cover and braise slowly for about 30 minutes.
Sprinkle the endives with the sugar or agave syrup and place under the broiler for 5 minutes.
To serve, drizzle with the lemon juice and olive oil and sprinkle with the finely chopped juniper berries.

Tip: This recipe can also be made with radicchio, if you like its bitter taste.

ENDIVES WITH A PARSLEY CRUST

SERVES 4

PREPARATION TIME 30 MINUTES

- 8 endives
- $1/2$ stick (3 tablespoons/50 g) salted butter
- Sea salt, freshly ground black pepper, and freshly grated nutmeg
- 1 teaspoon ground coriander

For the parsley topping:
- 12–15 flat-leaf parsley sprigs, finely chopped
- 8 Thai basil leaves, finely chopped
- 3 tablespoons of whole-wheat breadcrumbs
- 1 teaspoon Dijon mustard
- Zest and juice of 1 lemon

Using a sharp knife, remove the hard, cone-shaped core from the base of the endives.
Heat the butter in a large pan and sweat the whole endives. Season with salt, pepper, nutmeg, and the ground coriander. Add enough hot water to just cover the bottom of the pan ($1/5$ in./5 mm). Cover the pan and simmer for 10 minutes over a low heat.
To make the parsley topping, mix the chopped parsley and basil with the breadcrumbs, mustard, and lemon zest and juice, ideally in a blender or food processor. Season with salt and pepper. Drain the endives, cut them in half lengthwise and spread each half with the parsley mixture.
Place under a preheated broiler for 2 minutes, being careful to avoid browning the topping.

Tip: This parsley topping (*persillade*) can also be used to season vegetarian dishes and herb salads.

Skate with Beets and Capers

SERVES 4

PREPARATION TIME 30 MINUTES

- 4 portions of skate wing, each weighing about 8–12 oz. (230–350 g)
- 3 lb. 5 oz. (1.5 kg) beets, diced and cooked
- 1 white celery stick, peeled and diced into 1/4 in. (6 mm) pieces
- 1/2 stick (2 oz./60 g) butter
- 1 large shallot, finely chopped
- 1 garlic clove, finely chopped
- 16 capers
- 1 teaspoon honey
- Scant 1/2 cup (100 ml) raspberry vinegar
- Sea salt and freshly ground black pepper
- 8 sage leaves, chopped
- Leaves of 2 thyme sprigs
- 1 tablespoon olive oil
- Juice of 1/2 lemon

Chop half of the capers.
Blanch the celery in boiling salted water until al dente.
Heat a small piece of butter in a skillet and sweat the shallot and garlic. Add the chopped caper berries and beet and sauté for 5 minutes. Stir in the honey, sprinkle with the vinegar, and season with salt and pepper. Add the celery.
Cook the skate wings in 3 tablespoons (1 1/2 oz./40 g) of butter. Season with salt and pepper and sprinkle with the chopped sage and thyme. Drizzle with olive oil and lemon juice.
Serve with the beet, caper, and celery mixture, garnishing with the remaining capers.

Tip: Steamed potatoes are a good accompaniment for this dish.

Black Salsify with Juniper Berries and Sage

SERVES 4

PREPARATION TIME 30 MINUTES

- 12 black salsify roots
- Scant 1/2 cup (100 ml) vinegar
- 2 small pieces of butter
- 1 shallot, finely chopped
- 1 garlic clove, finely chopped
- 8 juniper berries
- 1 1/4 cups (300 ml) vegetable stock
- Sea salt and freshly ground black pepper
- 12 sage leaves
- 1/4 cup (60 ml) extra virgin olive oil

Wash the black salsify roots and peel them using a vegetable peeler.
Put them in a bowl, cover them with water, and add the vinegar. Set aside.
In a large pan, heat a small piece of butter and sweat the shallot and garlic. Cut the salsify roots to fit the dimensions of the pan, if necessary, and add them to the pan along with the juniper berries. Pour in the vegetable stock. Season to taste with salt and pepper.
Simmer, uncovered, over a low heat until the salsify is just al dente. Turn them occasionally to ensure that they cook evenly. Remove the salsify and keep warm. Reduce the stock by two-thirds. Strain this sauce into a bowl and whisk in the remaining small piece of butter.
Fry the sage leaves in a little olive oil, then drain and pat dry on paper towel. Season with salt and pepper.
Arrange the black salsify in a serving dish, pour over the sauce, and sprinkle with the crispy sage leaves.

Tip: The salsify roots are soaked in vinegar to prevent the flesh from reddening and especially to reduce the unpleasant nature of the latex that the roots release when peeled.

Facing page: A forgotten root vegetable that's a treasure of taste, salsify takes a long time to clean and, although it's a dirty job, it's well worth the effort. Whether peeled and roasted or boiled or steamed, salsify is a great alternative to traditional root vegetables.

Above, bottom: The end result: cleaned and prepared salsifies.

SPINACH AND TOMATO QUICHE

SERVES 8

PREPARATION TIME 1 HOUR 20 MINUTES

- 2 lb. 3 oz. (1 kg) fresh spinach
- 10 ^{1}/$_2$ oz. (300 g) fresh tomatoes, peeled and coarsely chopped
- 1 small piece of butter
- 1 large onion, chopped
- 2 garlic cloves, chopped
- 2 carrots, peeled and coarsely chopped
- 1 celery stalk, coarsely chopped
- 1 leek (white part only), coarsely chopped
- 2 tablespoons tomato paste
- 6–8 fresh basil sprigs, chopped
- ^{1}/$_2$ cup (^{3}/$_4$ oz./20 g) chopped fresh tarragon leaves
- Sea salt and freshly ground black pepper
- 2 cups (1 pint/500 ml) vegetable stock
- 8 eggs
- Scant ^{1}/$_2$ cup (100 ml) soy cream
- Scant ^{1}/$_2$ cup (100 ml) whole milk
- 1 sheet of puff pastry (8 oz./230 g), to fit an 11-in./28-cm pie plate
- ^{1}/$_4$ cup 1 ^{3}/$_4$ oz./50 g) grated Parmesan

Clean and rinse the spinach. Plunge into a pan containing ^{1}/$_2$ in. (1 cm) boiling water for a few minutes, then transfer to iced water to stop the cooking process. Pat the leaves dry then chop them coarsely.
To make the tomato sauce, heat the butter in a pan, add the chopped onion and garlic, and sweat for a few minutes. Add the chopped carrots, celery, and leek to the pan, and stir in the tomato paste. Cook over a gentle heat for 3 to 5 minutes.
Add the chopped tomatoes, basil, and tarragon and pour over the stock. Simmer for 20 minutes.
Meanwhile, preheat the oven to 350°F (180°C/gas 4).
Puree the sauce using a hand-held blender or in a food processor. Season with salt and pepper.
In a bowl, mix together the eggs, soy cream, and milk. Add the tomato sauce and beat lightly.

Line an 11 in. (28 cm) pie plate with parchment paper, then with the pastry. Prick the pastry all over using a fork. Arrange the spinach leaves over the pastry and pour over the tomato and egg mixture. Sprinkle with grated Parmesan and bake in the oven for 30 minutes.

PUY LENTILS WITH MINT

SERVES 4

PREPARATION TIME 30 MINUTES

- ^{3}/$_4$ cup (5 ^{1}/$_2$ oz./160 g) Puy lentils
- 10 fresh mint leaves, chopped
- 1 teaspoon cumin seeds
- 1 teaspoon mustard seeds
- 1 teaspoon chopped fresh turmeric
- ^{1}/$_2$ teaspoon ground cinnamon
- 3 tablespoons extra virgin olive oil
- 1 large shallot, chopped
- 1 garlic clove, finely chopped
- 1 bay leaf
- 1 ^{1}/$_4$ cups (300 ml) vegetable stock
- Scant ^{1}/$_2$ cup (100 ml) soy sauce
- Scant ^{1}/$_2$ cup (100 ml) cider or wine vinegar
- Sea salt and freshly ground black pepper

Rinse the lentils thoroughly in cold water and drain.
In a small skillet, dry-fry the cumin and mustard seeds, the chopped fresh turmeric, and the ground cinnamon.
Heat the oil in a pan and sweat the shallot and garlic. Once translucent, add the bay leaf and the lentils.
Cook for a further few minutes, then add the toasted spices, the stock, and the soy sauce.
Cover and simmer over a low heat until the lentils are cooked (about 15 to 20 minutes).
Remove the pan from the heat and let stand, covered. Season with salt, pepper, and vinegar.
Just before serving, add the fresh mint.

Tip: These lentils may also be served cold as a salad.

Herb Soup with Root Parsley

SERVES 4
PREPARATION TIME 30 MINUTES

- 2 tablespoons yellow lentils
- 1 tablespoon butter
- 1 onion, coarsely chopped
- 1 garlic clove, finely chopped
- 1 white celery stalk, coarsely chopped
- 1 leek, coarsely chopped
- 3 cups (1 $^1/_2$ pints/700 ml) vegetable stock
- 2 small roots of root parsley
- 10 Italian parsley sprigs
- 1 $^3/_4$ oz. (50 g) chervil
- $^3/_4$ oz. (20 g) fresh tarragon
- 3 $^1/_2$ oz. (100 g) spinach leaves
- Sea salt and freshly ground black pepper
- Juice of $^1/_2$ lemon

Rinse the lentils in cold water and drain.
Heat the butter in a pan and sweat the
onion, garlic, celery, leek, and lentils. Pour
in the stock and simmer for 15 minutes.
Meanwhile, wash the root parsley and cut
into thin ($^1/_8$ in./3 mm) slices. Cook in
boiling salted water until al dente (5 to
6 minutes).
Wash and pat dry the parsley, chervil,
tarragon, and spinach and add to the soup
pan. Bring to a boil, then remove the pan
from the heat. Puree using a hand-held
blender or in a food processor.
Strain the soup if you wish, and keep it
warm. Season with salt and pepper to
taste and add a squeeze of lemon juice.
Serve the soup in bowls or soup plates
with the slices of root parsley.

Note: Root parsley resembles parsnip in
many respects, but is smaller and has a
more delicate taste. Its leaves are similar
to those of flat-leaf parsley.

> " SHE CREATES A DIALOGUE BETWEEN THE LOCAL SEASONAL INGREDIENTS— OFTEN FROM HER OWN GARDEN—AND HER ARRANGEMENTS FEATURING SPRAYS AND BLOOMS; THE COMBINATION ALWAYS SEEMS SO NATURAL AND EFFORTLESS.
>
> *Lorraine Letendre*

Red, yellow, green, orange, and brown leaves line an avenue of trees and hedges in the park. It's important to use the natural colors and textures of the environments we live in to offer guidance for recipes, table decoration, and food presentation. Be on the lookout for colors that offer inspiration and take clues from the weather and the season when creating menus. During autumn's slow transition to colder temperatures, I often turn to food that helps warm the body, such as soups and cooked vegetables and grains. A particularly useful ingredient throughout the season, lentils are a versatile choice as they easily adapt the flavor and seasoning from other dishes. They are also low in fat, and in calories, and free from cholesterol. In addition to their valuable nutritional content, I also love to use lentils because they are quick and easy to prepare.

LENTIL AND TOMATO SOUP

SERVES 4
PREPARATION TIME 30 MINUTES

- $^1/_2$ cup (3 $^1/_2$ oz./100 g) yellow lentils
- 4 tomatoes, chopped
- 1 carrot
- 1 leek (white part only)
- 1 white celery stalk
- 1 small piece of butter
- 1 onion, chopped
- 1 garlic clove, finely chopped
- $^1/_2$ teaspoon cumin seeds
- $^1/_2$ teaspoon curry powder
- 2 cups (1 pint/500 ml) vegetable stock
- 8 sage leaves
- 1 tablespoons extra virgin olive oil
- Sea salt and freshly ground black pepper
- Scant $^1/_4$ cup (50 ml) sour cream

Trim and peel the carrot, leek, and celery. Wash and coarsely chop them.
Heat the butter in a pan and sweat the onion, garlic, and chopped tomatoes.
Wash and drain the lentils, then add them to the pan with the cumin seeds and curry powder. Pour in the stock and simmer gently for 20 minutes.
Meanwhile, gently sauté the sage leaves in olive oil until crispy.
Puree the soup using a hand-held blender or in a food processor, then strain if wished. Season with salt and pepper.
Serve in soup plates topped with a tablespoon of sour cream and some crispy sage leaves.

PAGES 138–139: Molten Chocolate Cake with Ganache, Pear, and Pear Sorbet (see recipe page 140). Patrick and I created the composition based on a black and white menu theme, and here it's combined with Korean pottery and a white squash. I adore squash for the decorative shape and the natural artistry of its appearance.
ABOVE, TOP: In an alabaster bowl, two truffles are waiting to be featured in a meal.

MOLTEN CHOCOLATE CAKE WITH GANACHE, PEAR, AND PEAR SORBET

SERVES 12

PREPARATION TIME 75 MINUTES

For the candied orange:
- 2 oranges
- $^1/_3$ cup (2 oz./60 g) caster sugar
- Scant 1 cup (200 ml) water
- Juice of 1 lemon

For the chocolate ganache:
- 1 $^1/_3$ cups (9 oz./250 g) chocolate chips (70 percent cocoa)
- Scant 1 stick (3 $^1/_2$ oz/100 g) unsalted butter, diced
- 5 eggs, separated
- $^1/_3$ cup (2 1/4 oz./65 g) brown sugar
- $^1/_4$ cup (1 oz/25 g) all-purpose flour

To serve:
- 12 scoops of pear sorbet
- 3 pears
- Juice of $^1/_2$ lemon

Preheat the oven to 350°F (180°C/gas 4). To make the candied orange, remove the peel from the oranges using a vegetable peeler and chop them finely. Wash them thoroughly. Blanch the peel for 20 seconds in 2 cups (1 pint/$^1/_2$ liter) boiling water and repeat this process five times, changing the blanching water and rinsing the peel under running water after each blanching.

Put the peel in a pan with the sugar and a scant cup (200 ml) of water and boil until the water has completely evaporated. Add the lemon juice.

To make the chocolate ganache, place the chocolate chips in a bowl over a pan of simmering water until melted. Add the butter and keep warm.

In a bowl, whisk the egg yolks with half of the brown sugar until pale and fluffy (ribbon stage). Add to the melted chocolate, along with the flour and candied orange peel.

Whisk the egg whites until stiff, adding the remainder of the brown sugar toward the end, while continuing to whisk.

Carefully fold the egg whites into the chocolate mixture. Set aside half of this ganache in a small bowl. Put the remainder into a piping bag fitted with a wide nozzle. Cover a baking sheet with baking paper and pipe small circles (about 2 in./5 cm diameter) of ganache onto it. Bake in the preheated oven for 7 minutes. To serve, place a chocolate cake on a plate, pipe a thin layer of ganache on top, add a scoop of pear sorbet, and decorate with slices of fresh pear sprinkled with a little lemon juice.

DRIED FRUIT COMPOTE WITH ORANGE

SERVES 4

PREPARATION TIME 40 MINUTES

- 12 organic dried apricots
- 2 tablespoons lemon zest
- 12 pitted prunes
- 8 dried figs
- 3 tablespoons raisins
- 1 small piece of butter
- 1 large cinnamon stick
- 1 tablespoon grated fresh gingerroot
- 2 star anise
- 1 tablespoon coriander seeds, toasted and crushed
- 1 $^1/_4$ cups (300 ml) orange juice
- Juice of 1 lemon

Chop the apricots into $^1/_4$ in. (6 mm) pieces. Put them in a small pan with the lemon zest and enough water to cover the bottom of the pan. Cover and cook over a low heat for 10 minutes.

Heat the butter in a skillet and briefly sauté all the dried fruits. Stir in the spices and cook for a further few minutes. Pour in the orange juice and continue to cook over a medium heat for 10 minutes. Just before removing the pan from the heat, add the lemon juice. Let cool, then refrigerate.

Tip: Serve for breakfast, or to accompany a plain or chocolate cake.

BAKED APPLES WITH BLUEBERRIES

SERVES 4

PREPARATION TIME 30 MINUTES

- 4 red apples (e.g., Fuji)
- 2 ³/₄ oz. (80 g) blueberries
- 4 teaspoons butter
- ¹/₂ teaspoon ground cinnamon
- Scant ¹/₂ cup (100 ml) agave syrup
- ¹/₂ teaspoon ground aniseed
- Juice of 1 orange

Preheat the oven to 350°F (180°C/gas 4).
Cut a ¹/₂-in. (1-cm) thick section off the
top of each apple, retaining the stalk.
Using an apple corer, remove the cores.
Place the apples in a baking pan. Put
1 teaspoon of butter inside each one
and sprinkle with the cinnamon. Replace
the apple "lids" and bake in the preheated
oven for 15–20 minutes.
Meanwhile, heat the agave syrup and
ground aniseed in a small frying pan until
slightly caramelized.
When the syrup has begun to turn gold,
add the blueberries and orange juice, and
cook over a medium heat for a further
3 or 4 minutes.
Remove the apples from the oven and
pour the blueberries and their juice over
them.

Tip: This is a perfect accompaniment for
roast poultry or game.

WINTER

Bright conversation. A warm, crackling fire. Dim lights. A room illuminated with candles. The Dutch word *gezelligheid* captures the emotional feeling of warmth garnered from a pleasant, enjoyable experience. It's an emotion I feel throughout the year, particularly in winter, a special season for appreciating the pleasures of family and home. We spend the holidays in the mountains in Verbier, Switzerland, and there the kitchen is the center of life. When appetites yearn for heartier food, roasted root vegetables such as celeriac are favorites, both for the taste and for their health benefits. Candlelight is more important this season, so choose a variety of heights and shapes to add dimension and glow. While adding a burst of color from flowers—such as amaryllis, which is perfect for the season—it's important to balance the eye with softer and more muted colors, such as white pumpkins and other natural, monochrome objects to create harmony.

FACING PAGE: Winter sets in and colder temperatures ease the orchard into a season of hibernation. I love living in a climate with four distinctive seasons. It offers the chance to appreciate the natural beauty and character of each season, even in the chilly months.

RIGHT: Although we don't often cook with an open fire, the heat from the flame and charcoal is ideal for keeping dishes warm in between courses, such as roasted carrots and potatoes with herbs.

PAGES 144–145: We spend several weeks every winter in the mountains of Verbier, Switzerland. When we arrive at the chalet, I like to do one big shopping trip to have a wide variety of winter ingredients on hand to offer hearty menu options needed for energy in higher altitudes.

CABBAGE STUFFED WITH SQUASH

SERVES 4

PREPARATION TIME 30 MINUTES

- ¹/₄ Savoy cabbage
- 1 small butternut squash
- 1 carrot
- 3 ¹/₂ oz. (100 g) celeriac
- 1 tablespoon goose fat
- 1 large shallot, finely chopped
- 1 garlic clove, finely chopped
- Sea salt, freshly ground black pepper, and freshly grated nutmeg
- Scant 1 cup (200 ml) vegetable, chicken, or game stock

Preheat the oven to 325°F (160°C/gas 3). Remove the outer leaves from the cabbage. Blanch them for 30 seconds in boiling salted water. Refresh them in iced water, then drain. Set aside.
Coarsely chop the remainder of the cabbage. Peel and coarsely chop the butternut squash, carrot, and celeriac. Heat the goose fat in a large pan and sweat the shallot and garlic. Add the chopped vegetables and pour over the stock. Season with salt, pepper, and nutmeg.
Cover the pan and simmer over a medium heat for 20 to 25 minutes. Stuff the blanched cabbage leaves with the cooked vegetable mixture, folding the leaves to form small packages. Place them in a roasting pan and cook in the oven for 15 minutes.
Cut them into several pieces and arrange them in a serving dish with Duck Leg Confit (see p. 162).

BABY BEET SALAD WITH CILANTRO

SERVES 4

PREPARATION TIME 30 MINUTES

- 16 baby beets with their leaves
- Scant 1 cup (200 ml) vegetable stock
- 1 teaspoon coriander seeds
- 2 cloves
- 4 juniper berries
- 1 thyme sprig
- 1 sage sprig
- Sea salt and freshly ground black pepper
- 3–4 tablespoons extra virgin olive oil
- 1 shallot, finely chopped
- 1 garlic clove, finely chopped
- 4 sucrines
- Scant ¹/₄ cup (50 ml) red wine or sherry vinegar
- 4 fresh cilantro sprigs, finely chopped

Peel the beets and cut them in half, keeping the leaves intact if possible. Cook them until al dente (about 15 minutes) in the vegetable stock with the coriander seeds, cloves, juniper berries, thyme, sage, salt, and pepper. Heat a little oil in a pan and sweat the shallot and garlic for a few minutes. Cut each sucrine into several slices. Wash and pat dry.
In a bowl, toss together the salad, shallots and garlic, beet, olive oil, vinegar, and cilantro. Season with salt and pepper.

FACING PAGE: Stuffed cabbage is a healthy way to appeal to winter appetites that yearn for homemade comfort food.
ABOVE: I'm often drawn to ingredients that are delicious and beneficial to the body. Beet contains high levels of potassium, magnesium, and iron, and is a good source of vitamins for helping to boost the immune system. This is ideal in winter. A natural source of antioxidants, protein, and carbohydrates, beet is perfect for salads and side dishes.

> " THERE'S NO STANDING ON CEREMONY
AT THE VERVOORDTS'—SIMPLY A WARM
AND FRIENDLY WELCOME. MAY'S
EASY MANNER AND GENEROUS HOSPITALITY
MAKES YOU FEEL NURTURED.

Apollonia Poilâne

On a winter table in the late afternoon is a vegetable juice based on fennel. The recipe requires the use of the entire vegetable, including the bulb and leaves. Combine the fennel with celery, zucchini, parsley, and green apple in a juicing machine with a slow extractor to create a healthy juice that's a great start to any menu. There are many great juicing machines available and it's helpful to research their technical specifications to choose one that suits the needs of the kitchen best. How fast the machine operates and how easy or hard it is to clean the machine are important considerations.

CREAMED BUTTERNUT SQUASH BRUSCHETTA WITH GINGERROOT AND HAZELNUT CRUMBLE

SERVES 4

PREPARATION TIME 35 MINUTES

- 10 $^1/_2$ oz. (300 g) butternut squash
- 1 sweet potato
- 1 small carrot
- $^1/_3$ cup (80 ml) extra virgin olive oil
- 1 shallot, finely chopped
- 1 garlic clove, finely chopped
- $^1/_2$ teaspoon ground turmeric
- $^1/_2$ teaspoon curry powder
- Scant 1 cup (200 ml) vegetable stock
- 1 tablespoon finely chopped fresh gingerroot
- 12 slices of multigrain baguette
- 2 tablespoons hazelnut oil
- 1 tablespoon ($^1/_3$ oz./10 g) shelled whole hazelnuts
- Sea salt and freshly ground black pepper

Peel the butternut squash, sweet potato, and carrot and cut them into $^1/_2$ in. (2 cm) pieces.
Heat 2–3 tablespoons of olive oil in a large skillet and brown the shallot and garlic. Add the diced sweet potato, carrot, and butternut squash.
Sprinkle over the turmeric and curry powder and pour in the vegetable stock. Simmer until the stock has evaporated. Add the finely chopped gingerroot, then puree. Strain, then let cool.
Drizzle the bread slices with olive oil, season with salt and pepper, and broil under the broiler.
Heat the hazelnut oil in a small skillet and gently fry the hazelnuts with some salt and pepper until golden. Coarsely chop the hazelnuts with a knife.
Spread each slice of toast with a little butternut squash puree and garnish with chopped hazelnuts. Season with salt and pepper.

Tip: This squash puree can be served with fish or meat.

WINTER VEGETABLE SALAD WITH PUMPKIN SEEDS

SERVES 8

PREPARATION TIME: 40 MINUTES

- 1 large yellow turnip
- 1 large white turnip
- 1 large round black radish
- $^1/_8$ celeriac
- 1 small kohlrabi
- 2 apples (Golden Delicious or Pink Lady)
- $^1/_2$ cup (120 ml) extra virgin olive oil
- 2 tablespoons pumpkin seeds
- 1 large shallot, chopped
- 1 tablespoon chopped fresh lemongrass
- 1 tablespoon chopped fresh gingerroot
- 8 fresh mint leaves, finely chopped
- 2 tablespoons chopped fresh flat-leaf parsley
- Juice of 1 lemon
- 1 tablespoon Dijon mustard
- Sea salt and freshly ground black pepper

Peel and julienne (cut them into matchstick-size strips) the vegetables and apples.

Heat a little oil in a small pan and fry the pumpkin seeds until golden. Season with salt and pepper.

Sweat the shallot, lemongrass, and gingerroot in a pan with a tablespoon of olive oil.

Put all the julienned vegetables into a large bowl with the mint leaves and chopped parsley, then add the pumpkin seeds.

To make the dressing, mix together the remaining olive oil, the lemon juice, and mustard, and season to taste with salt and pepper.

Pour the dressing over the salad and toss gently.

Serve in individual bowls or in a serving dish.

ROASTED ROOT VEGETABLES WITH SAGE

SERVES 8

PREPARATION TIME: 45 MINUTES

- 4 yellow turnips
- 4 white turnips
- 4 small carrots
- 1 rutabaga
- 8 small parsley stalks
- 2 shallots, finely chopped
- 2 garlic cloves, finely chopped
- 16 sage leaves
- $^1/_2$ cup (120 ml) extra virgin olive oil
- 3 tablespoon virgin hazelnut oil
- 2 teaspoons honey
- Sea salt and freshly ground black pepper
- Juice of 1 lemon

Preheat the oven to 300°F (150°C/gas 2). Peel the turnips, carrots, and rutabaga and cut in half or quarters, so all pieces are of similar size or weight. Chop the parsley stalks.

Put the vegetables and parsley in a roasting pan and add the shallots, garlic, four of the sage leaves, the parsley, olive and hazelnut oils, and the honey. Season with salt and pepper.

Place in the oven for 35 minutes. Shake the vegetables in the pan regularly.

Heat a little oil in a small pan and fry the remaining 12 sage leaves until crispy. Season with salt and pepper.

Remove the vegetables from the oven and sprinkle them with the lemon juice. Add the sage leaves and serve.

ABOVE: Roasted root vegetables with sage. This is a superb winter side dish to accompany slowly roasted chicken or other slow-cooked meat.

LAMB CASSEROLE

SERVES 8

PREPARATION TIME 3 HOURS 15 MINUTES

- Two 4 lb. 6 oz. (2 kg) lamb shoulders, boned and tied
- 4 cloves
- 4 juniper berries, chopped
- Sea salt and freshly ground black pepper
- 1 large piece of butter
- 4 unpeeled shallots
- 4 unpeeled garlic cloves, crushed
- 8 sage leaves
- 4 thyme sprigs
- 4 bay leaves
- 2 rosemary sprigs
- 4 $^1/_4$ cups (2 pints/1 liter) chicken stock
- Scant 1 cup (200 ml) soy sauce
- 4 white turnips (each approx. 2 in./5 cm long)
- 4 yellow turnips (each approx. 2 in./5 cm long)
- 4 carrots
- 2 fennel bulbs
- 1 lb. 2 oz. (500 g) pumpkin flesh, diced

Preheat the oven to 325°F (160°C/gas 3). Season the lamb shoulders with cloves, juniper berries, pepper, and a little salt. Heat the butter in a large casserole and brown the lamb shoulders on all sides, along with the shallots, and garlic. Add the sage, thyme, bay leaves, and rosemary.

Deglaze the casserole and pour in the stock and soy sauce. Cover and roast in the preheated oven for 1 $^1/_2$ hours. (The meat should reach a temperature of 140°F/60°C.)

Meanwhile, peel the turnips and carrots. Cut turnips in half, the carrots into quarters, and the fennel bulbs into eight equal-size pieces. Add to the casserole and cook for a further 1 $^1/_2$ hours. Remove the meat and vegetables from the casserole and keep warm.

Filter the cooking juices and pour them into a pan with the pumpkin flesh. Cook for 10 minutes, then puree using a hand-held blender or in a food processor.

Pour this sauce over the meat and vegetables to serve.

Note: This casserole can also be cooked over a very low heat on the cooktop. The advantage of oven roasting, however, is that the temperature can be set, remains stable, and the heat is evenly distributed.

Baked Celeriac with Nuts and Grains

SERVES 4–6

PREPARATION TIME 2 HOURS

- 4 × 10 ¹/₂–14 oz. (300–400 g) young celeriac
- 2 tablespoons extra virgin olive oil

For the seed sauce:

- 1 tablespoon sunflower seeds
- 1 tablespoon pumpkin seeds
- 1 tablespoon flaxseed
- 1 tablespoon pine nuts
- 1 tablespoon chopped hazelnuts
- 1 tablespoon chopped parsley
- 1 tablespoons extra virgin olive oil
- 1 tablespoon virgin hazelnut oil
- 1 teaspoon sherry vinegar
- Sea salt, freshly ground black pepper, and freshly grated nutmeg

Preheat the oven to 225°F (110°C/gas 1/4). Wash and scrub the celeriac and put in a roasting pan. Cook in the oven for 2 hours.

Meanwhile, make the seed sauce: in a skillet, dry-fry the sunflower and pumpkin seeds, flaxseed, pine nuts, and chopped hazelnuts until they are lightly golden. Remove them from the pan to stop them cooking further.

Chop them finely, let cool, then put them in a bowl and stir in the parsley, olive and hazelnut oils, and sherry vinegar. Season to taste with salt and pepper.

When cooked, remove the celeriac from the oven. Peel, cut in half, and arrange on a serving plate. Drizzle with olive oil and sprinkle with nutmeg.

Serve with the seed sauce.

White Radish with Cumin

SERVES 4

PREPARATION TIME 15 MINUTES

- 30 white radishes
- 1 teaspoon cumin seeds
- 1 ¹/₄ cups (300 ml) vegetable stock
- Scant ¹/₄ cup (50 ml) extra virgin olive oil
- Sea salt, freshly ground black pepper, and freshly grated nutmeg
- 1 small piece of butter
- 1 lemon

Using a vegetable peeler, peel the radishes, keeping about 1 in. (2.5 cm) of their stems.

Heat a skillet and dry-fry the cumin seeds, then add the radishes and stock. Cook over a gentle heat, just below simmering point, for 8 minutes.

Using a slotted spoon, remove the radishes from the cooking liquid. Heat the oil in a skillet and brown the radishes lightly. Season to taste with salt, pepper, and nutmeg. Keep warm.

Meanwhile, reduce the cooking liquid by two-thirds, then whisk in the butter using a hand-held whisk or blender. Place the radishes in a serving dish, drizzle with lemon juice, and pour over the reduced stock.

Tip: You can use this same recipe with a mixture of different root vegetables, such as carrots or turnips. Serve as an accompaniment to lamb, roast chicken, or game.

PAGES 152–153: Next to a window in the cellar, a collection of Japanese winter squash known as kabocha, or green pumpkin, is placed alongside beetroot and wooden carving boards. I adore them for their shape and color. If eaten, kabocha have a very hard skin and a slightly sweet taste, and offer a rich source of beta-carotene and vitamins.

BABY ONIONS GLAZED WITH LEMON AND TURMERIC

SERVES 4

PREPARATION TIME: 30 MINUTES

- 14 oz. (400 g) small white onions, peeled
- 1 tablespoon clarified butter (or ghee)
- Scant $^1/_2$ cup (100 ml) agave syrup
- 1 tablespoon dried thyme
- $^1/_2$ tablespoon cumin seeds
- $^1/_2$ tablespoon mustard seeds
- 2 untreated lemons, chopped into small pieces
- 1 tablespoon chopped fresh turmeric
- $^1/_2$ teaspoon curry powder
- $^1/_2$ cup (60 ml) extra virgin olive oil
- Sea salt and freshly ground black pepper

In a pan, sweat the onions in the clarified butter or ghee, then add the agave syrup, thyme, and a dash of water. Cover the pan and cook gently for 15 minutes. Dry-fry the cumin and mustard seeds in a small skillet.
Add the chopped lemons, the chopped fresh turmeric, and the curry powder. Sauté for 2–3 minutes then add the olive oil.
Remove the pan from the heat and add the mixture to the onions.
Season with salt and pepper.

ABOVE, TOP: Placed in a small, wooden bowl, a selection of dried herbs, including thyme and sage, is a very versatile mixture. Patrick and I use this specific blend to make herbal tea infusions, which is an ideal after-dinner drink and a relaxing way to end the evening. The same mixture is wonderful to use as seasoning and produces excellent flavor, particularly with poultry.

SQUAB WITH YELLOW TURNIPS

SERVES 4

PREPARATION TIME 30 MINUTES

- 8 squab fillets
- $^1/_4$ cup (60 ml) extra virgin olive oil
- 1 white onion, finely chopped
- 2 garlic cloves, finely chopped
- 16 small yellow turnips (2–2 $^1/_2$ in./5–6 cm. diameter), peeled and quartered
- Sea salt and freshly ground black pepper
- Scant 1 cup (200 ml) vegetable or chicken stock
- 6 flat-leaf parsley sprigs, finely chopped
- 2 lovage leaves, finely chopped
- Juice of $^1/_2$ lemon
- 1 tablespoon cumin seeds, lightly toasted
- 1 tablespoon clarified butter (or ghee)

Preheat the oven to 350°F (170°C/gas 4). Heat the olive oil in a pan and sweat the onion and garlic.
Add the turnips and season. Pour in the stock, bring to a boil, then reduce the heat and simmer over a gentle heat until nearly all the liquid has evaporated.
Add the parsley, lovage, lemon juice, and toasted cumin seeds. Keep warm. Melt the clarified butter or ghee in a skillet and brown the squab on both sides. Transfer to a roasting pan and place in the oven to cook for 5 minutes.
Remove the squab from the oven, cover with aluminum foil, and let rest for 10 minutes.
Arrange the turnips and squab fillets on a serving dish.

Note: The yellow turnip is one of those forgotten vegetables, like the rutabaga, with which it is easily confused.

BUTTERNUT SQUASH WITH WINTER VEGETABLES

SERVES 4

PREPARATION TIME 45 MINUTES

- 1 small butternut squash (about 1 lb. 5 oz./600 g)
- 2 tablespoons (³/₄ oz./20 g) mixed seeds (pumpkin, sunflower, pine nuts)
- Sea salt and freshly ground black pepper
- 2 cups (1 pint/500 ml) vegetable stock
- 1 bay leaf
- 1 yellow carrot
- 1 orange carrot
- 1 small parsnip
- 1 small root of root parsley
- ¹/₄ cup (1 ³/₄ oz./50 g) green lentils, washed and drained
- 2–3 tablespoons extra virgin olive oil
- 1 shallot, finely chopped
- 1 garlic clove, finely chopped
- ¹/₄ cup (2 oz./60 g) Creamed Butternut Squash (see p. 120)
- 3 tablespoons cider vinegar
- 1 tablespoon chopped fresh flat-leaf parsley

In a skillet, dry-fry the seeds. Season with salt and pepper and chop them with a knife. Set aside.

Peel the squash and cut into 4 slices about ¹/₂ in. (1 cm) thick. Pour the stock into a pan and add the bay leaf and salt and pepper. Cook the squash slices in the stock until al dente (3–4 minutes). Remove the slices using a slotted spoon (reserving the stock) and cut them to size using a 3-in. (8-cm) plain round cookie cutter.

Peel the root vegetables and dice them into ¹/₄ in. (6 mm) pieces. Cook them in the reserved stock until al dente (4–5 minutes). Remove using a slotted spoon, then cook the lentils in the same stock for about 20 minutes.

Heat the oil in a large pan and sweat the shallot and garlic, then add the root vegetables and lentils and sauté rapidly for a few minutes. Season with salt and pepper and stir in the vinegar and parsley. Reheat the Creamed Butternut Squash on a low heat in a non-stick frying pan. To serve, lay a butternut squash round on each plate, spread some creamed butternut squash on top, then divide the vegetables and chopped seeds between each serving.

Tip: For a professional finish, place the cookie cutter over the butternut squash base and add the other ingredients before removing it carefully.

JERUSALEM ARTICHOKE SOUP WITH WINTER TRUFFLES

SERVES 4

PREPARATION TIME 30 MINUTES

- 1–2 tablespoons hazelnut oil
- 1 large white onion, coarsely chopped
- 1 leek (white part only), coarsely chopped
- 1 celery stick, coarsely chopped
- 10 Jerusalem artichokes
- 4 ¹/₄ cups (2 pints/1 liter) vegetable stock
- Sea salt and freshly ground black pepper
- Scant 1 cup (200 ml) truffle juice (see tip)
- 1 ¹/₂ oz. (40 g) winter truffles, thinly sliced

Heat the hazelnut oil in a pan and sweat the onion, leek, and celery, without browning.

Set aside 2 Jerusalem artichokes and peel and cut into large dice the remainder. Add to the pan.

Add the stock, bring to a boil, then cover the pan, reduce the heat, and simmer for 15 minutes.

Puree the soup using a hand-held blender or in a food processor and then, if you wish, strain it.

Season to taste with salt, pepper, and the truffle juice.

Peel the remaining Jerusalem artichoke and slice thinly. Garnish the soup with the raw Jerusalem artichoke and winter truffle slices.

Tip: To make your own truffle juice, put the truffles in a glass jar, cover with grapeseed oil, and leave to infuse for a day.

PAGES 158–159: On a magical, misty morning, the moat offers a reflection of the courtyard above that's like a mirror to display the colors and textures of the moment.

ABOVE, TOP: A quarter section of Poilâne bread sits on a cutting board ready to be served at sunrise for breakfast.

Above, top: With a light dusting of snow, the hedges in the garden are viewed in both the shadow and light of the winter sun. During this season in particular, it's important to remember that comfort food—which warms the body from the inside—can also be healthy food, providing warmth and sustenance without extra calories.

Roast Chicken with Lemon and Herbes de Provence

SERVES 4

PREPARATION TIME: 40 MINUTES

- 2 lb. 10 oz. (1.2 kg) chicken (preferably black leg)
- 2 unpeeled shallots
- 2 garlic cloves, crushed
- $\frac{1}{2}$ untreated lemon
- 4 thyme sprigs
- 1 rosemary sprig
- 6 fresh sage leaves
- 2 tablespoons extra virgin olive oil
- Sea salt and freshly ground black pepper

Preheat the oven to 400°F (200°C/gas 6). Stuff the chicken with the whole shallots, crushed garlic cloves, lemon, thyme and rosemary sprigs, and sage leaves.
Season the chicken inside and out and rub the olive oil into the skin.
Put the chicken into a roasting pan and place into the preheated oven.
After 10 minutes, reduce the temperature to 325°F (160°C/gas 3) and cook for a further 25 minutes, basting occasionally. Remove the chicken from the oven and let rest, covered (with aluminum foil, for example), for 10–15 minutes before serving.

Tip: The shallots roasted in their skins can be served as an accompaniment to the roast chicken.

Duck Leg Confit

SERVES 4

PREPARATION TIME 1 HOUR 40 MINUTES

- 4 wild duck legs
- 10 $\frac{1}{2}$ oz. (300 g) goose fat
- Sea salt and freshly ground black pepper
- 1 garlic clove, crushed
- 2 juniper berries, crushed
- 2 cloves
- 1 thyme sprig
- 2 bay leaves
- 10 peppercorns, crushed

Heat a tablespoon of goose fat in a large pan and brown the duck legs. Season with salt and pepper.
Add the remainder of the goose fat along with all the other ingredients. Cover the pan and place over a very low heat for 1 $\frac{1}{2}$ hours. The temperature should reach 140–160°F(60–70°C); the fat should not boil.

Tip: Retain the goose fat and store in a pot in the fridge for future use. It can be reused four or five times. Simply strain the hot liquid fat. When it has solidified, remove the fat, which will have formed a layer over the cooking juices, and put into pots.

Spelt Risotto

SERVES 4
PREPARATION TIME 50 MINUTES
(PLUS 12 HOURS SOAKING)

- 7 oz. (200 g) spelt
- 1 teaspoon mustard seeds
- $^1/_2$ teaspoon ground cinnamon
- $^1/_2$ teaspoon cumin seeds
- $^1/_2$ teaspoon coriander seeds
- $^1/_2$ teaspoon ground cardamom
- $^1/_2$ teaspoon ground turmeric
- Scant $^1/_4$ cup (50 ml) coconut oil
- 1 large shallot, finely chopped
- 1 garlic clove, finely chopped
- 1 kaffir lime leaf
- 1 tablespoon chopped fresh gingerroot
- Scant 1 cup (200 ml) coconut milk
- Scant 1 cup (200 ml) passata (sieved tomato pulp)
- 4 small turnips
- Juice of $^1/_2$ lemon
- Sea salt and freshly ground black pepper
- 4 tablespoons ricotta

Soak the spelt in cold water for 12 hours. Rinse until the water runs clear.
In a casserole, dry-fry the spices, then add the coconut oil, shallot, and garlic and cook for 3 minutes. Add the spelt, kaffir lime leaf, and gingerroot and cook for a further 2 minutes.
Pour in the coconut milk and passata, then cover and simmer for 10 minutes. Meanwhile, peel the turnips and dice into $^1/_2$ in. (1 cm) pieces. Add them to the pan and continue to simmer for a further 10 minutes. If necessary, add a little water. Add the lemon juice and season with salt and pepper. Just before serving, carefully stir in the ricotta.

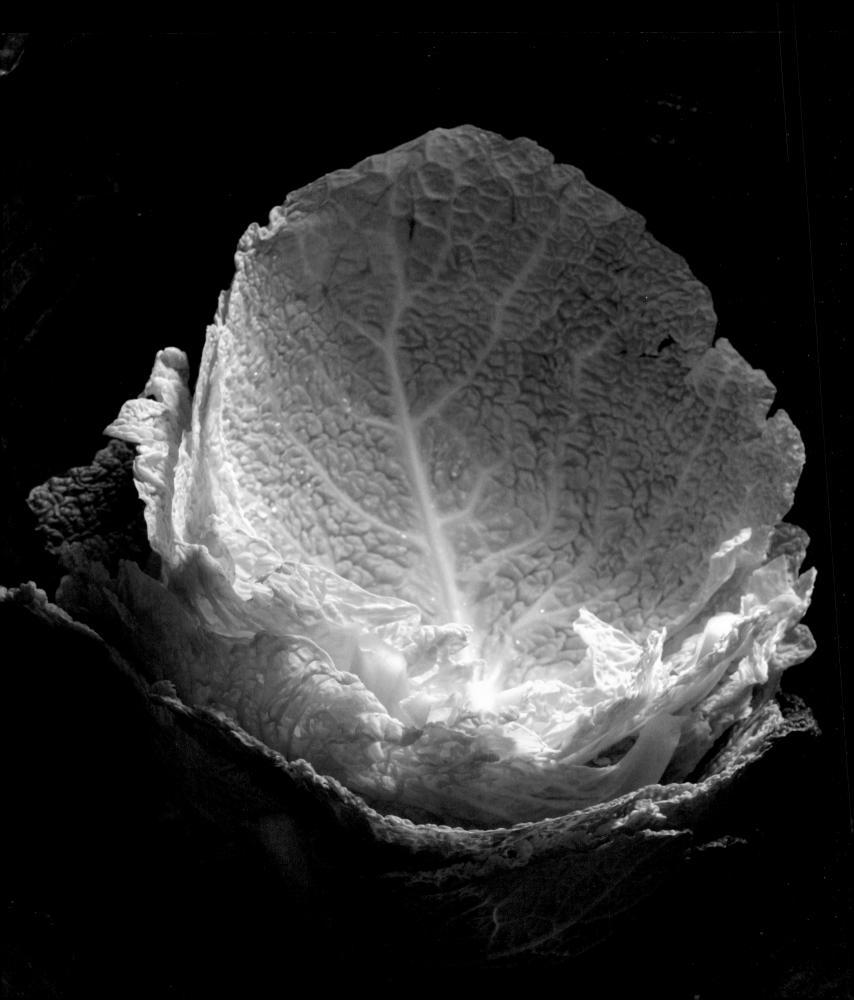

PAGES 164 AND 165: The delicate texture and natural beauty of cabbage leaves reminds me of the powdery petals of a flower in full bloom. Enjoying a meal together is about sharing, and a family-style serving of stuffed green cabbage with pumpkin and sage and slowly cooked wild duck is a pleasant reminder of that.

ABOVE, TOP: The season's last apples and pears from the orchard are placed in a favorite basket.

VEAL FILLET WITH SAVOY CABBAGE

SERVES 4

PREPARATION TIME 1 HOUR

- 1 lb. 12 oz. (800 g) veal fillet (or 1 boneless rib roast)
- 1/2 Savoy cabbage
- 2 small pieces of butter
- 1 shallot, finely chopped
- 1 garlic clove, finely chopped
- 3 1/2 oz. (100 g) pumpkin, cut into 1/4 in. (1/2 cm) pieces
- 6 juniper berries, chopped
- Sea salt, freshly ground black pepper, and freshly grated nutmeg
- 7 oz. (200 g) ground veal
- 1 whole egg plus 1 egg yolk
- Scant 1/2 cup (100 ml) soy cream
- 1 tablespoon pumpkin seeds
- 1 tablespoon pine nuts
- 1 3/4 oz. (50 g) caul fat
- 2 tablespoons extra virgin olive oil

Set aside a few tender green cabbage leaves and slice the remainder finely. Blanch the whole cabbage leaves in boiling salted water for a few minutes, then pass them under cold running water and set aside to drain on absorbent kitchen paper.
Heat a small piece of butter in a large skillet and sweat the shallot and garlic. Add the chopped cabbage, diced pumpkin, and juniper berries and simmer for 15–20 minutes, then season to taste with salt, pepper, and nutmeg.
Meanwhile, preheat the oven to 300°F (140°C/gas 2).
Mix the ground veal, the egg and egg yolk, and the soy cream together in a food processor.
Place this mixture and the cooked vegetables in the fridge for 5 minutes, then mix them together.
Cut the veal fillet in half lengthwise and cover the two halves with this stuffing mixture. Sprinkle with the pumpkin seeds and pine nuts. Bring the two fillets together to enclose the filling. Wrap the

veal fillet in the reserved blanched cabbage leaves, then wrap the whole package tightly in the caul fat.
Heat the remaining small piece of butter with the olive oil in a skillet and gently brown the stuffed cabbage.
Place in a roasting pan and transfer to the oven to cook for about 35 minutes. Remove from the oven, cover with aluminum foil, and leave to rest for 10 minutes.
Cut into slices to serve.

RED CABBAGE WITH APPLES AND STAR ANISE

SERVES 8–10

PREPARATION TIME 50 MINUTES

- 1 red cabbage
- 6 Jonagold apples
- 1/2 stick (1 3/4 oz./50 g) butter
- 4 medium red onions, finely chopped
- 4 star anise
- 2 cinnamon sticks
- 1 teaspoon ground aniseed
- Scant 1/2 cup (100 ml) agave syrup
- 2 tablespoons palm sugar
- Scant 1 cup (200 ml) raspberry vinegar
- Freshly ground black pepper and freshly grated nutmeg

Finely shred and wash the cabbage. Peel, core, and quarter the apples.
Heat the butter in a pan and sweat the onion until transparent. Add the shredded red cabbage, apple quarters, star anise, cinnamon sticks, and ground aniseed. Cover and cook over a low heat for 20 minutes. If necessary, add some water to prevent sticking.
Add the agave syrup, palm sugar, and vinegar and cook for a further 20 minutes. Season to taste with freshly ground black pepper and nutmeg.

> **"WHAT DO I LIKE BEST AT MAY'S?
> EVERYTHING! THOUGH I MUST SAY
> THAT I HOLD LASTING MEMORIES
> OF BREAKFASTS THAT WERE HARD
> TO BREAK OFF, WITH HER BOILED
> BLUE EGGS, TOAST, DELICIOUSLY
> SCENTED HONEYS, AND HOMEMADE JAMS.**
>
> *Gautier Capuçon*

From early morning to late evening, the kitchen in Verbier is the true heart of our home in the mountains. The days and nights that we spend there during the Christmas holidays include important family moments. Here, the breakfast table in the chalet appeals to all appetites and includes a selection of bread, fruit, compote, quinoa, oats, and yogurt. Baskets and cutting boards are efficient and decorative ways of setting the table quickly. We often drink green tea or hot water with lemon and ginger to start the morning. Usually our longest meal of the day, we like to linger at the table enjoying each other's company and gathering much-needed nutrition and energy.

PEARS WITH CITRUS FRUITS AND CINNAMON

SERVES 4
PREPARATION TIME: 30 MINUTES

- 4 small pears (e.g., Comice)
- 1 orange or 2 mandarins, untreated
- 1 untreated lemon
- 2 cups (500 ml) water
- 1 cinnamon stick
- 1 tablespoon chopped fresh gingerroot
- 1 pinch of saffron powder
- Scant $^1/_2$ cup (100 ml) agave syrup or rice syrup

Peel the pears and cut them in half lengthwise. Cut the orange (or mandarins) and lemon into $^1/_4$-in. (5-mm) thick strips, with the skin. To make the syrup, put 2 cups (500 ml) water into a small pan and bring to a boil. Add the cinnamon stick, gingerroot, saffron, lemon and orange strips, and the agave syrup, and let infuse for 10 minutes. Poach the pears in this liquid, heated to 175–195°F (80–90°C), for 10 minutes. Remove the pan from the heat and leave the pears to cool in the pan. Remove the pears from the pan and strain the juice. Pour this strained juice over the pears to serve.

Tip: Serve these pears with a chocolate dessert, or with muesli for breakfast.

ORANGE AND SPICE SAUCE

SERVES 4

PREPARATION TIME 15 MINUTES

- 1 teaspoon finely chopped fresh orange zest
- 1 star anise
- 1 cinnamon stick
- 2 cardamom pods
- 1 teaspoon coriander seeds
- Scant 1 cup (200 ml) fresh orange juice
- 1 teaspoon finely chopped fresh gingerroot
- 1 teaspoon finely chopped Thai lemongrass
- 1 teaspoon vanilla instant pudding mix, or cornstarch or potato starch

Blanch the chopped orange zest for 20 seconds in a little boiling water and repeat this process five times, changing the blanching water and rinsing the zest under running water after each blanching. In a skillet, dry-fry the star anise, cinnamon stick, cardamom pods, and coriander seeds until golden. Add the orange juice, blanched orange zest, and the chopped gingerroot and lemongrass. Bring to a boil, then remove from the heat and leave to infuse for 5 minutes. Dissolve the vanilla instant pudding mix in a teaspoon of cold water, and use to thicken the sauce.

MOLTEN CHOCOLATE CAKE WITH ALMONDS AND CRANBERRIES

SERVES 12

PREPARATION TIME 45 MINUTES

- 9 oz. (250 g) dark chocolate (min. 70 percent cocoa)
- 4 eggs
- 1 cup (7 oz./200 g) palm sugar
- 2 1/4 sticks (9 oz./250 g) butter, softened
- 3 cups (9 oz./250 g) ground almonds
- 1/2 cup (2 1/2 oz./75 g) dried cranberries
- Cocoa powder, for dusting

Preheat the oven to 350°F (180°C/gas 4). Line a 9 in. (23 cm) cake pan with baking parchment. Melt the chocolate in a bowl over a pan of boiling simmering water. Whisk the eggs with the sugar (in a food processor if wished) until white and fluffy (ribbon stage).

Melt the butter in the melted chocolate, then stir both into the egg and sugar mixture, along with the ground almonds and dried cranberries, to form a smooth, glossy mixture.

Pour into the lined cake pan and bake in the oven for 30 minutes.

Remove the cake from the oven, unmold, and let cool.

Dust with cocoa powder to serve.

HAZELNUT AND NOILLY PRAT CHOCOLATES

MAKES 40 CHOCOLATES

PREPARATION TIME 45 MINUTES (INCLUDING RESTING TIME FOR THE PASTRY)

- 10 1/2 oz. (300 g) finely chopped hazelnuts
- 3 1/2 oz. (100 g) granulated sugar
- Scant 1/2 cup (100 ml) thick sour cream
- Scant 1/2 cup (100 ml) Noilly Prat
- 1 puff pastry sheet (8 2/3 oz./245 g)
- 3 1/2 oz. (100 g) dark chocolate (min. 70 percent cocoa)
- 3 tablespoons (1 oz./30 g) almonds, finely chopped
- 3 tablespoons (1 oz./30 g) unsalted pistachios, finely chopped
- 1/3 cup (1 oz./30 g) shredded coconut

Preheat the oven to 325°F (160°C/gas 3). In a pan, caramelize the sugar with a dash of water until it is golden brown in color. Add the chopped hazelnuts, the cream, and the Noilly Prat. Stir to mix and heat until the liquid has reduced by half.

Place the puff pastry sheet onto a baking sheet and cover it with the hazelnut caramel. Place in the oven for 15 minutes. Let cool then place it in the freezer for at least 2 hours.

Melt the chocolate in a bowl over a pan of boiling simmering water.

Mix together the chopped almonds and pistachios and shredded coconut and spread out on a plate.

Using a large knife, cut the frozen preparation into 1/2 in. (1 cm) squares. Using a fork, dip the squares into the melted chocolate, then immediately lay each chocolate-covered square onto the chopped nut and shredded coconut mixture to coat. Place in the fridge until set.

Tip: You can substitute walnuts or pecans or a mixture of these for the hazelnuts.

Note: Noilly Prat is a French brand of vermouth, created in 1813.

INDEX OF RECIPES

ACKNOWLEDGMENTS

"One cannot think well, love well,
sleep well, if one has not dined well."
Virginia Woolf

For their contributions to this book, I would like to thank my husband Axel, my children Boris and Dick, and my family.
For many years, they have offered their kind patience and discerning palates and have often been the first to try the recipes contained
in this volume. Their direct answers, constructive encouragement, and appreciation taught me many useful lessons about refining
ingredients and creating dishes.

I'm very grateful to Patrick Vermeulen and I would like to thank him for his hard work and for everything he does. In the kitchen,
he is my right hand.

Thank you to Jean-Pierre Gabriel and his entire team. His professional eye and devotion brought the recipes to life.

Thank you to Michael Gardner for putting into words what I could never write down myself.

Thank you to the gardeners at s'Gravenwezel for the many vegetables and gifts they cultivate in the garden.

Thank you to Anne-Sophie Dusselier for her precious help in coordinating the various contributors to the creation of this book.

Thank you to Ghislaine Bavoillot and the team at Flammarion. She encouraged me to do the book and without her
I would never have embarked on such an ambitious project.

Thank you to the many friends who have expressed their enjoyment of dinners with us at s'Gravenwezel, in particular Ina Garten,
Donna Leon, Dries Van Noten, Katia Labèque,
Melinda Blinken, Marielle Labèque, Martine Dornier, Robert Carsen, Lorraine Letendre, Apollonia Poilâne,
and Gautier Capuçon, whose kind words grace these pages.

May Vervoordt

Page 22 © Heinz Mack, *Dynamische Struktur*, signed and dated "Mack 60/61" (on the back). Oil on canvas, 42 ½ × 51 in. (108 × 130 cm).
Page 29 © Jef Verheyen, *Blauwe Lichtstroom*, 1970. Matte varnish on canvas, 71 × 71 in. (180 × 180 cm). ADAGP, Paris 2012.

Recipes translated from the French by Anne McDowall   Editorial Direction: Ghislaine Bavoillot   Design: Isabelle Ducat
Copyediting: Penelope Isaac   Typesetting: Gravemaker+Scott   Proofreading: Chrisoula Petridis
Color Separation: IGS   Printed in Italy by Canale

Simultaneously published in French as *A la table de May: Tables et recettes au fil des saisons chez Axel et May Vervoordt*
© Flammarion, S.A., Paris, 2012

English-language edition
© Flammarion, S.A., Paris, 2012

12 13 14   3 2 1

ISBN: 978-2-08-020110-2

Dépôt légal: 09/2012